HAUNTED ARIZONA TRI-CITIES

CHANDLER, MESA & TEMPE

DEBE BRANNING

HAUNTED America

Published by Haunted America
A Division of The History Press
Charleston, SC
www.historypress.com

Copyright © 2024 by Debe Branning
All rights reserved

First published 2024

Manufactured in the United States

ISBN 9781467158183

Library of Congress Control Number: 2024937575

This book is dedicated to the girls and leaders of Girl Scout Troop 89 of Omaha, Nebraska; Troop 1477 of Mesa, Arizona; and Troop 3092 of Mesa, Arizona. Being a part of these Girl Scout troops opened my eyes to the importance of history and living the adventure. It also taught me that research and integrity are some of the most important parts of life—and death.

CONTENTS

ACKNOWLEDGEMENTS

I would like to thank the many historians from the towns of Chander, Mesa and Tempe who graciously shared their knowledge of some of the most exciting tales from these historic central Arizona towns, e-mailed me newspaper clips and photographs and pointed me in the direction of citizens with personal experiences. Jennifer Merry was always supportive and answered my many questions so that these tales could be as historically accurate as possible.

A big shout-out to all the paranormal investigative teams, tour guides, tour companies and location owners who shared their experiences, data logs and stories of the unknown to fill these pages with the spooky phenomena they have encountered over the years.

I thank my paranormal team and personal paranormal friends who have accompanied me to explore the spirits and mysteries of the Tri-Cities buildings. Kudos to all who helped with photography and to Vanna Chisamore for her edits to the manuscript.

Again, my wish is for other paranormal enthusiasts to hop in their vehicles and explore the spirits encountered in these historic cities and towns before they become misty memories of the past. And as always, I will add, "History and mystery go hand in hand!" Carry on the tradition!

The grand opening of Tri-City Mall in Mesa. *Courtesy of AZCentral.com.*

INTRODUCTION

The thirty-third parallel has long been associated with the Freemason fraternity. Masons and other occultist groups revere the number 33 above all others. Many acts of war, murder and violence have taken place on or near the thirty-third parallel. Strangely enough, the Tri-Cities of Tempe, Mesa and Chandler were all established along the ley lines of the thirty-third parallel, and this could be one of the reasons these towns have such high energy levels and unexplained amounts of paranormal activity.

The thirty-third parallel is circle of latitude that is thirty-three degrees north of the Equator. It brings with it an energy that manifests in powers and abilities for those of us who seek out its god of prosperity or abundance.

Ancient Egyptians lived on the thirty-third parallel, as did those in the ancient Orient and Israel. The Mayan culture, along with their Native American counterparts, were closer to the Equator, but still, they were influenced by the powers of the thirty-third parallel. You can follow the thirty-third parallel and its ley line through Arizona. Note how it travels through the Tri-Cities of Tempe, Mesa and Chandler.

1

CHANDLER

HIGH-TECH OASIS OF THE SILICON DESERT

The community of Chandler was founded by Dr. A.J. Chandler on May 16, 1912. Dr. Chandler, the first veterinary surgeon for the Territory of Arizona, purchased eighty acres of land from the federal government south of Mesa in the Salt River Valley in 1891.

Dr. Chandler began to study the new science of irrigation engineering and was instrumental in developing an early system of canals in what was then a vast, dry desert. In the early 1900s, Chandler owned an 18,000-acre ranch. The charter of the Salt River Project provided that each landowner could acquire water to irrigate only 160 acres. Dr. Chandler sought help from local planners and architects to subdivide his ranch and drew up a townsite map. Chandler began to nationally advertise the sale of Chandler Ranch sites.

Chandler opened the townsite office on May 17, 1912. Suddenly, excursion trains on the new Arizona Eastern Railroad brought in three hundred buyers who spent $50,000 on land purchases that day.

The boomtown consisted of three wooden buildings—the townsite office, a dining hall and the Morrison Grocery Store. A billboard marked the spot where the elegant Hotel San Marcos was later erected. It is said Dr. Chandler had an ambitious plan that was way ahead of its time. His vision included a landscaped central park that would be surrounded by the town's businesses. The walkways in front of the buildings would be covered by a trellis-like roof that would provide much-needed shade. The deed restrictions required landowners to begin construction on their land within one year.

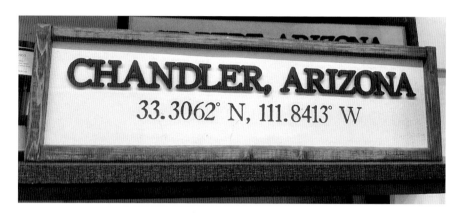

Chandler is along the thirty-third parallel (33.3062). *Author's collection.*

It wasn't long before Chandler started to look like an established town. Businesses were built along the west and south sides of the central park and featured the Bank of Chandler and a new Eastern Railroad Depot. Dirt roads bordered the park, and soon, wagons and Model T Fords moved about the growing town. The park flourished in green grass and newly planted trees. It was eventually divided into north and south sides by the Commonwealth Canal.

A huge celebration was held with the grand opening of the Hotel San Marcos on November 22, 1913. Its guests included Governor George P. Hunt and Vice President Thomas Marshall. The elegant hotel was an immediate success, with visitors from all over the country coming to explore the new state of Arizona.

Agriculture continued to be the big business in Chandler. Its primary crops were cotton, grains and alfalfa, while farmers and ranchers raised cattle, sheep and ostriches, as ostrich feathers had become popular in women's fashions.

In 1920, Chandler boasted over one thousand residents. Roads were paved, and water and sewer services were ready for updated systems. Dr. Chandler was nominated to serve as the first mayor until one could be elected. The Great Depression was not devastating for most of Chandler's residents. The cotton crash of 1920 had a far greater impact on the agriculturally focused town. Dr. Chandler did not do well during the Depression years either. The Bank of Chandler collapsed, and sadly, Dr. Chandler lost the San Marcos to his creditors. Chandler was able to retire comfortably and lived in a cottage on the grounds of his dream hotel.

Downtown Chandler. *Courtesy of Pinterest.*

In the late 1930s, Chandler began to experience problems prompted by growth and technology. The drivers of new automobiles didn't realize Arizona Avenue then ended at the town plaza. These fast-paced cars tended to jump the curb and then land smack dab in middle of the park. Large diesel trucks that made deliveries to businesses around the park began having trouble navigating the narrow roads that bordered the plaza. So, in 1940, the state proposed to align Route 87 with Arizona Avenue. Angry residents were reluctant to watch their treasured park be divided in half for a highway, although the original design was no longer safe or practical.

Dr. Chandler passed away on May 8, 1950. On May 24, 1954, Chandler was upgraded from a town to a city. In recent years, Chandler's city limits have expanded for miles, and the population has exploded from 30,000 in 1980 to more than 240,000 today. While agriculture is still a vital element of the town's economy, Chandler enjoys a strong manufacturing and electronics sector as well.

The downtown storefronts have been restored to modern versions of their original turn-of-the-century looks, and the plaza has been redesigned and proudly named after the city's founder. Family festivals, such as the Ostrich Festival, and other annual events make Chandler a popular stop for winter visitors and locals alike. Dr. Chandler's spirit and energy lives on in his desert oasis!

CROWN PLAZA SAN MARCOS RESORT
1 SAN MARCOS PLACE
CHANDLER, AZ 85224

Arthur Burnett Benton, an architect from Southern California, designed the San Marcos Resort in downtown Chandler. Benton was an authority on California mission design. The San Marcos is the best example in Arizona of a completely integrated Mission Revival design. This landmark hotel was the vision of wealthy landowner Dr. A.J. Chandler. He chose its site in the town he founded and which bears his name in 1912. Dr. Chandler named the resort San Marcos after Friar Marcos DeNiza, who is said to have visited the Chandler area in 1539 while searching for the mythical "Seven Cities of Cíbola."

The hotel opened in 1913 to a crowd of five hundred that included the governor of Arizona, congressmen and the vice president of the United States. It was the first resort in Arizona to boast amenities such as golf, tennis, horseback riding and polo. Palm Springs in California had not yet been developed, and because of its out-of-the-way location, the San Marcos played host to the powerful and famous. The resort was originally conceived as a prime winter getaway for celebrities, dignitaries and movie stars.

The resort's famous guests have included Herbert Hoover, Bing Crosby, Clark Cable, Fred Astaire, Rex Allen, Joan Crawford, Errol Flynn, Jimmy Stewart, Gloria Swanson and many more. Chicago mobster Al Capone once had a room in one of the bungalows that were added west of the main building. The hotel promised the most modern in efficient accommodations, such as incandescent light bulbs and telephones in every room. When it opened, the San Marcos Hotel was the only electrified building in Chandler. There were beautiful gardens, walks and pools separating its grounds.

The resort sits at the Chandler Townsite on the northwest corner of San Marcos Place and Commonwealth Avenue and faces east onto San Marcos Plaza, the center of Chandler. It was added to the National Register of Historic Places on April 27, 1982. In 1986, the restoration of the original building and the construction of 250 new rooms began. The property reopened in 1987 as the Sheraton San Marcos Resort. It is now operated by InterContinental Hotels Group's Crowne Plaza brand; the hotel is owned by Interwest Capital after having been acquired in 2013.

The MVD Ghostchasers paranormal team and two members of the AZ Paranormal Investigations team did an investigation of the San Marcos

Top: The San Marcos Hotel opened in 1913. *Courtesy of the* Mesa Tribune.

Bottom: Historic San Marcos Hotel in Chandler. *Courtesy of the* Mesa Tribune.

Hotel one fall evening in 2004. Their cameras captured a strange light anomaly in the lobby, where guests see Dr. Chandler crossing the room. They also picked up the presence of energy on the second floor and were able to follow a flowing, cool breeze as it shot along the indoor balcony.

Many of the hotel's office personnel claim they have seen Dr. Chandler roaming the hallways where the hotel offices are located. A few employees have reported feeling a strong presence of a man near or behind their shoulders. When they turn to look, no one is there. The offices are located on the historic second floor, where the meeting rooms are also located. Locked doors will suddenly open. Chandeliers will swing, and a ghostly opera singer will serenade the halls. One of the employees once stuck his hand into the darkened Clark Cable Room and reached around the door to lock it. He felt something stroke his hand. He froze and then shoved the door open to look inside. The room was empty. The hotel's front desk receives strange calls from extensions that do not exist. A female apparition has been seen, and the moaning of a male spirit has been heard.

One of the security guards took the paranormal investigators to a secret stairway that led to the hotel's basement and its mysterious tunnels. A rickety, steep ladder led them to the dark basement. They needed flashlights to work their way through the cluttered storage area. This old, seldom-used cellar was not for the faint-hearted. It is said that Chicago gangster Al Capone used this passageway to reach the tunnels that once whisked the rich and famous to the bungalows along the golf course. The group trekked through dead bugs, broken holiday decorations, sludge and things they did not want to shine a flashlight on until they finally reached the tunnels. As true as a good Geraldo Rivera TV special, the tunnels had been cemented over and their secrets sealed forever. The group recorded more energy in the basement, and there was definite spirit activity throughout the dreary catacombs.

Back upstairs, the MVD Ghostchasers lined up on the lobby staircase for their traditional group picture. They always invite any photogenic spirits to join in the shoot. Later, when the film was developed, there was a glowing light reigning over the group. They had no doubt that it was the good doctor joining them in the photograph.

Jamie Veik of the Phoenix Arizona Paranormal Society (PAPS) wrote,

The San Marcos Hotel in downtown Chandler has quite a bit of activity in the century that it has been around. Tons of celebrities have stayed at the resort, including presidents, and with this kind of history, paranormal activity is sure to be around. We investigated the boiler room in the basement in 2016 and captured tons and tons of EVPs; EMF activity and disembodied voices were always present. We were unable to decipher who or what is hanging around down there, but we believe there are multiple entities. In one of the offices on the second floor, a vacant one at the time we were there, several EVPs were captured, weird electronic phenomenon with our equipment and personal phones took place, and a few of the investigators even believed that they witnessed a shadow figure in the hallway right outside of the room, where a woman has been spotted over the years. They believe that is the spirit of a woman who jumped from the second floor back in its glory days. Just while walking around, there were periods of uneasy feelings amongst the team, and one of the most incredible EVPs captured on camera was in a common area, in which a female voice is screaming, "HELP!"

Left: The San Marcos staircase with an image of Dr. Chandler. *Author's collection.*

Below: A modern view of the Crown Plaza San Marcos Resort. *Author's collection.*

The San Marcos is still one of the top resorts in the Tri-Cities area, but beware, some of the vacationing time travelers have not bothered to check out of this relaxing oasis!

THE OSTRICH SPEAKEASY
10 NORTH SAN MARCOS PLACE NO. B1
CHANDLER, AZ 85225

Andrew Fishburn is a manager at the San Marcos Hotel, one of the original buildings in Chandler, constructed by Dr. A.J. Chandler himself. And the rumor is true: underneath the resort hotel are a series of tunnels that stretch out in all directions.

Fishburn recently led a group of visitors on a tour beneath the hotel's restaurant. After Fishburn unlocked a plywood door and escorted them down the stairs, the group was soon in the middle of the basement. On the other side was a dark stone room.

"The rumors say that the tunnels down here were used to transport booze, women, even ostriches, and…bodies!" Fishburn explained. "I believe it's true!

Some Arizona residents don't realize it, but ostriches were one of the main reasons Chandler exists. It sounds bizarre, but Chandler is known for its annual Ostrich Festival each spring. Dr. Chandler was a veterinarian and a rancher. At one time, there was not much in Chandler aside from his luxurious hotel resort and his ranchland, which was populated by ostriches. During the Victorian and Edwardian eras, ostrich feathers were all the rage in women's fashion. Dr. Chandler assumed ostrich feathers would soon become the next big thing in 1920s flapper fashions. Sadly, that did not go according to his plan.

When the tunnels were rediscovered in the basement of the hotel, it is said a box of ostrich feathers were found hidden away there. Michael Merendino heard the story when he began seeking out the perfect location for a new bar.

Merendino adopted the ostrich feather story and decided to convert a section of the forgotten basement tunnels into the Ostrich Bar, a vintage-looking speakeasy-style bar hidden under the San Marcos Hotel. Some folks began to assume it may had been a speakeasy at some point.

Others believe the Chandler tunnels had a less-than-reputable side to them. They believe they were likely used for smuggling in alcohol during

The Ostrich
Speakeasy in
the San Marcos
basement.
Courtesy of Yelp.

Prohibition. The hotel operated during the Prohibition years, miles and miles away from any of the large cities in Arizona at the time. Rich people traveled from miles around to stay at the luxury hotel and were entertained with the finest liquors and wines in the area.

As they were in all the grand hotels in the desert, tunnels were used in a more practical way at the San Marcos Hotel. The tunnels moved cooling air through the buildings in the summertime, and they were also used to move warm air into the enormous buildings during the chilly winter months.

The San Marcos Hotel had what was then the largest heating system in the Tri-City area. It had a massive fuel tank embedded in the concrete underneath it. This fuel tank generated so much heat that the hotel used some of its tunnels to transfer the heat to other neighboring buildings. The boiler has long since stopped being used for heating. But since it is so large and heavy, it is impossible to remove. It remains in the basement to this day.

There is another story told that says the basement of the San Marcos Hotel was used for animal cremations. Dr. Chandler was a veterinarian—the only vet for many miles in any direction. This meant he might have had to administer cremation services for the animals he treated in the early 1900s.

Fishburn said, "They would bring coal, ice and remains into the basement. The crematorium was installed next to the boiler, and the ash pit is still visible. It was built to cremate animals, but I suspect it was probably used for a person or two."

The tunnels are now walled up in place, and others have been filled in. One tunnel dead ends at the hotel's swimming pool. The tunnel that the Ostrich Bar is built on continues to the other side of the bar's bricked-up wall. It is now nearly impossible to explore the tunnels and what remains in them. They will live on as one of the San Marcos Hotel's greatest secrets.

But what about these ostriches that Chandler is known for? Did you know that at one time, Arizona had its very own Rodan?

Back in the late 1950s or early 1960s,

The doorway to the Ostrich Speakeasy. *Author's collection.*

some readers will remember the thrill of staying up late on Saturday night and watching the science fiction movie classics—scaring ourselves half to death! The movie monster featured in *Rodan* (1956) emerged from a giant egg found underground in a mountainside near Mount Aso. The large bird grew horns and had a wingspan of two hundred meters. It was not until he was finally conquered and destroyed that Earth was safe from his reign of terror.

Arizona once had its own version of Rodan, a violent and destructive ostrich by the name of Roughneck. Sadly, Roughneck, a male ostrich, had at least two human fatalities to his credit. While on a Phoenix ostrich farm, Roughneck had a reputation for being a vicious bird. One season, he killed one of the farmhands by crushing the man's chest with his powerful claw foot. Sometime later, he attacked another farmhand. The poor man was injured so severely that he died a short time later. The animal was decidedly ferocious and continuously attacked the farm workers as they entered the field. The bird's neck was lined with scars he received in various battles, hence his nickname, Roughneck.

The big, handsome, black-feathered ostrich was brought to Chandler in the fall of 1914 by Dr. Chandler from the Pan American Ostrich Farm just

A secret stairway to the Ostrich Speakeasy. *Author's collection.*

outside of Phoenix. Roughneck, with over two hundred other ostriches, was herded over land on a three-day trek from Phoenix, around South Mountain and over to the Chandler Ranch. People came from miles around to see the ostrich drive, and it was Roughneck that started a stampede. The stampeding ostriches frightened a passing horse that was pulling a buggy and caused the horse to bolt, throwing a woman out of the buggy and killing her.

Eventually, karma caught up with the killer ostrich. Roughneck wrapped his long, battle-scared neck around a strand of wire in his pen in such a way that he twisted his neck into a knot, cutting off his airway and slowly choking him to death. Yes, Roughneck hanged himself on a barbwire fence on March 22, 1915, and was found dead the next morning.

The bird was housed just west of Chandler, Arizona (the home of the current Ostrich Festival), and was part of the large flock owned by Dr. A.J. Chandler. Chandler stored ostrich feathers in the basement of the San Marcos Hotel until the ladies' fancy hat industry faded from existence during World War I.

The next time you attend one of those entertaining Ostrich Festivals, where guests dine on ostrich burgers and purchase ostrich oils, feather dusters and leather goods, keep in mind that some of these birds just might be a descendant of Roughneck. You've seen how the movie *Rodan* ends. Need I say more?

M-TRONIKS MUSIC STORE
571 NORTH ARIZONA AVENUE
CHANDLER, AZ 85225

This small electronics and music business was located in a small strip mall facility and was a popular stop for musicians in the valley for many years. The COPS (Crossing Over Paranormal Society) Crew were contacted to do an investigation of M-Troniks in 2017, due to some frightening events that repeatedly occurred at the location. The owner reported that on several occasions, the alarm had sounded in the middle of the night. There was never a sign of forced entry to the building. There were reports of objects moving, shadows, cold spots, disembodied voices and employees feeling they were being watched as they worked. After a recent remodel of the facility, the activity began to increase, as though the spirits had been awakened.

The M-Troniks building in Chandler. *Author's collection.*

The COPS Crew conducted several paranormal ghost hunts in two separate buildings at M-Troniks. Jay Yates investigated one of the rooms as his wife, Marie, sat outside and observed from a chair. Suddenly, she saw the door open slowly on its own.

They closed the door once again. A few minutes later, they both heard the doorknob jiggle, as if an unseen spirit was trying to open the door a second time. Marie continued to watch Jay through a glass window in the door. He said the room was breezy and seemed to pulsate. Every light on the K-2 meter was lit and blinking wildly. He began feeling dizzy and jumped back toward the wall.

"Did you hear that?" Jay asked in disbelief. "I heard a female whisper! She whispered my name. I heard her whisper, 'Jay!'" The investigator left the room, as he needed a breath of fresh air. They never learned the identity of the mysterious female spirit.

CURSED OBJECTS AT TERROR TRADER
941 WEST ELLIOT ROAD SUITE 3
CHANDLER AZ 85225

Are you ready to visit the spookiest showroom in the entire Tri-Cities area? From the outside, Terror Trader looks like your average strip mall venue—

plain and simple. That is, until you notice a coffin or a pair of gargoyles protecting the front entrance. Terror Trader is a unique horror collectible store that not only sells horror movie merchandise, books, posters and comics, but it also has a spooky collection of cursed objects on display in a special oddities room at the rear of the store.

Enter if you dare!

There are plenty of creepy, haunted or cursed items there, such as an old phonograph player that has been linked to the suicides of four women in the eastern United States. A record was found playing on the vintage phonograph at the discovery of each suicide. The music piece was donated to a Christian church that burned to the ground in a terrible fire. The only item that survived was the phonograph! One of the phonograph's previous owners decided to remove its needle from the needle arm, and things began to settle back to normal. The needle has not been replaced on the needle arm to this day.

Debe Branning and Megan Taylor pulled into the parking lot of Terror Trader and decided to make a visit to the store and its famed little room of horrors, which is technically a small museum within the store, filled with items owner Jason Swarr has collected over the years. Some of these items are merely on display, while other artifacts are for sale to collectors of oddities.

Manager Jason Swarr escorted the two ladies to the museum and smiled as he flipped on the lights so they could take in the wonderment of the wall-to-wall display of haunted dolls and toys and voodoo offering jars and a curio cabinet full of human skulls.

"This wall has my collection of vintage Ouija boards, but I don't play around with them! I was a skeptic for a long time until I watched my surveillance cameras capturing footage of items flying off the shelves with not a single living soul standing anywhere near them," Swarr told the two women. Some of the talking boards are vintage, from the 1940s and 1950s; the oldest board was made around 1905.

There is a handcrafted witch's tower that was built by an earth witch to ward off evil. The earth witch had been involved in an abusive relationship for over twenty years. She finally packed up her children and moved to Florida, never to return. Many years later, Swarr obtained the unusual item online. He nonchalantly placed it on a counter facing the east. Not long after the tower arrived, strange things began happening. There is a triangle crystal that rests in the window at the top of the tower. Swarr kept it set in the twelve o'clock position. However, every time he entered the oddities room, he

Above: Terror Trader in Chandler. *Author's collection.*

Left: Spooky Quija boards on Terror Trader's wall. *Courtesy of Megan Taylor.*

would find the crystal sitting in the two o'clock position. At first, he thought a customer of one of the staff members had moved it. But one day, he was there alone when, once again, he set the crystal to twelve o'clock. When he returned a short time later, it had changed to the two o'clock position.

Jason was baffled. He decided to contact the woman in Florida to see if she knew why the crystal would continually move on its own. The woman retold her unfortunate story of abuse and how she finally moved away and remained in Florida all these years.

"And where did you live before you moved to Florida?" he asked.

"Chandler, Arizona," she replied.

He was taken aback by her answer. "The Terror Trader shop is in Chandler!"

Now it made sense. The witch's tower was facing the east, still reaching out to the earth witch, and there was a two-hour time difference between them then. Jason moved the tower to a different end of the counter, where it faces the west, and now, the crystal stays in position.

What is a store with terror items without haunted dolls? Here, you will find a large collection of haunted dolls that have been donated by customers or collectors who were not comfortable with them in their homes. Customers purchase the haunted dolls, but some end up bringing them back! The store once had a crying doll that was heard weeping and was found in the middle of the floor several times. Employees ended up placing the doll in a sealed case, and it has since shed no more tears.

The store's cabinet filled with human skulls can be a little overwhelming. Inside, there is a skull of a man who was killed by an arrow. Some of the skulls and human bones were found underwater. The Haitian voodoo skull with the syncretism carving is said to be between 150 and 200 years old, and it has an uneasy energy surrounding it.

Other items in this museum that are on the darker side of things include a vintage electroshock therapy machine from the 1960s, a straitjacket, a 1900s mortician table, Voodoo altar jars from the 1920s, a machete from a head hunter and way too many other to list here.

Paranormal teams such as the UnFazed Crew, Grim Adventurer and many others have come in to Terror Trader to conduct investigations at the little shop of horrors—with unprecedented results. Some teams had no experiences at all, while others report their K-2 meters, RemPods and Ghost Box tools were active the entire night. Some have heard voices and drums in the shop when all else is quiet.

Terror Trader's skulls. *Courtesy of Megan Taylor.*

One of the teams investigating the store was McInville Paranormal with Donna Gerron, who said,

The group was in the front of the store, and they kept hearing a chime like the door was opening—but it was locked. The register and computer were turned off, so that could not have been it either. One of the investigators was asking questions, which made the little lighted cat balls show activity. The most interesting thing that happened was when I stood on the side of the store where the coffin and killer clown display is. Out of nowhere, we heard three loud bangs from the back of the store. Scared the crap out of everyone! The owner of the store ran out the back looking for someone playing a prank, but nobody was out there. It sounded as if someone was trying to break down the back door!

Without a doubt, there is a lot of deathly energy in the oddities room. Some folks fear the feeling of being watched or having a heavy sensation in their chest. Some walk away because they cannot breathe—and some are too scared to come back into the room ever again!

CHANDLER HIGH SCHOOL
350 NORTH ARIZONA AVENUE
CHANDLER, AZ 85225

The majestic Chandler High School is one of the oldest high schools in Arizona. The original high school opened its doors in September 1914, just two years after the city of Chandler was founded and Arizona declared statehood. The groundbreaking for the current building with a small gymnasium began in 1921. This is one of the oldest parts of the building and is affectionately referred to as Old Main. The building was constructed in a Classical Revival style by architects Allison and Allison. Orville A. Bell designed the current gymnasium in 1939. Both structures were placed in the National Register of Historic Places in 2007. The school's name obviously comes from the city's founder, Dr. Chandler.

Old Main seems to be the hottest site on campus for paranormal activity. Voices and ghostly apparitions have been experienced in the hallways on the second floor of the English building. Paranormal

A view of the front of Chandler High School. *Author's collection.*

sightings and disembodied voices are still experienced in the north wing of the historic building.

One student said, "I go to Chandler High School, and it is haunted. Sometimes, you can see a person looking out the window on the top floor of Old Main. Teachers say there is no basement in Old Main, but I found it—unfortunately, the door was locked. I saw a set of stairs going down, but then it went black, and I swear there was another door with a lock on it. I'm scared that the ghost might get angry one day with all the stories!"

Another concerned student added, "I just started going to Chandler High. My friend and I were heading to English class, and we entered through the door to Old Main on the far left. After we went inside, we saw two doors under the stairwell. One door was installed with a small window. I decided to take a quick peek, and I could see stairs going down, and boy, did it look creepy as hell! I noticed the door was the only one that had a different kind of lock on the outside door."

The number of people who have had paranormal experiences in the school is surprisingly high, and it includes teaching staff, students, parents, administrators, visitors and custodians, both former and current. The activity seems to be focused on the second floor of the school's north wing, which is noted as the oldest area on the campus.

One of the teachers felt the presence of a spirit standing nearby while she used the restroom in the faculty lounge, while another instructor witnessed a ghost enter the school auditorium, pause for a moment and then quickly exit out another door.

A janitor who has been employed at Chandler High School for almost thirty years admits he has encountered a male apparition five or six times in the hallways of the English building. Apparently, the building is so haunted

Chandler High School, built in 1921. *Courtesy of Pinterest.*

that at least one of the custodians has refused to clean that part of the building after they endured a spook encounter there.

MVD Ghostchaser Cindy Lee recalled attending a high school basketball game that was held at the gymnasium in the late 1969 or 1970. Cindy was not a student at the high school but often attended events with her friends. During halftime, the group of friends stepped outside to get a bit of fresh air and continue their socializing. Cindy wandered near the windows of the English building. While glancing upward, she noticed the figure of a man standing at the second-floor window with a soothing blue aura surrounding him.

"It reminded me of the color of the ocean," Cindy recalled. "I was looking high into the window and could only see his body from the waist up. I just remember it was a beautiful shade of blue. I kept watching until it finally faded away. It was then I learned I had observed the famous 'blue ghost' of Chandler High School."

GOODYEAR-OCOTILLO CEMETERY
GOODYEAR ROAD
CHANDLER, AZ 85248

The Goodyear-Ocotillo Cemetery is a small cemetery that holds a lot of Arizona's early history. It is a small plot of land nestled in the middle of a large housing community (Fulton Ranch) in the southern part of Chandler. The land surrounding this cemetery represents the beginning of commercial cotton growing in Arizona.

In January 1917, after World War I, the Goodyear Tire and Rubber Company founded the Southwest Cotton Company to begin producing

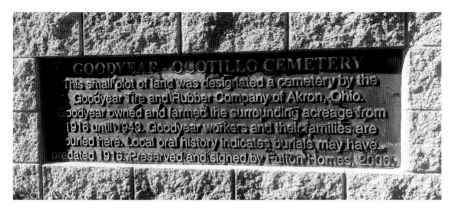

Goodyear-Ocotillo Cemetery sign. *Author's collection.*

long-staple cotton for domestic and miliary use. People came from across the United States and Mexico to start a new life in the cotton fields. Migrant workers and their labor laid the agricultural foundation of the east valley.

An inscription on the wall at the cemetery's entrance reads: "This small plot of land was designated a cemetery by the Goodyear Tire and Rubber Company of Akron, Ohio. Goodyear owned and farmed the surrounding acreage from 1916 until 1943. Goodyear Company workers and their families are buried here. Local oral history indicates some burials may have predated 1916."

When the cemetery was established in 1916, it was a part of the original town of Goodyear and the Goodyear Tire Company. Cotton was a huge crop in the area, and the tire company used the cotton inside of its tires. The cemetery contains the remains of more than two hundred Mexican Americans and Yaqui Natives who worked in the cotton fields.

Sadly, over the years, many of the name plaques have been lost or destroyed. The handmade grave markers have slowly fallen to despair or are now completely gone. Local community volunteers try to keep the cemetery clean and preserved. Thankfully, Fulton Ranch residents have remained reverent to the three-acre graveyard.

Many of the burials are those of children who died of diseases such as typhoid fever, pneumonia, dysentery and other childhood illnesses and were not attended by physicians at the time. Mothers died in childbirth and contracted unattended illnesses, and since many of them were coming from Mexico, they did not seek medical treatment. Fathers died from exhaustion or similar conditions caused by overworking. It was not an easy life for these immigrants.

Left: A grave marker in the Goodyear-Ocotillo Cemetery. *Author's collection.*

Below: A view of Goodyear-Ocotillo Cemetery. *Author's collection.*

Opposite: A grave marker with a heart in Goodyear-Ocotillo Cemetery. *Author's collection.*

Over time, Goodyear Tire's operations were moved to the west valley. At that time, the city was pretty much deserted, and the cemetery was all that was left. Many of the names on the grave markers have been lost, but many families still honor their loved ones with flowers and tributes. While many of these markers have no names, the hard work and sacrifice of these workers and immigrants are being venerated.

The Cahal Crew Paranormal group took an interest in the cemetery and decided to try to communicate with the souls of the primarily Hispanic cemetery. Using RemPods, Ghost Box devices and dowsing rods, the group began jotting down the names of the spirits that call the cemetery home. As they explored the rows of white crosses, their medium began pulling in the energy of a young mother who was weeping over the grave of her young daughter.

"She is sobbing in grief," she said, "She comes here often."

Debe Branning did a walk-through of the cemetery as she snapped photographs for this chapter of the book. She noted the eerie silence of the burial ground—not even the chirping of a bird could be heard. "They are at peace at long last," she noted.

2
MESA

GATEWAY CITY

Mesa is the most populous city in the Tri-City area. It is bordered by Tempe to the west and Chandler to the south. It was once the home to the Tri-City Mall, one of the first large department store malls in the East Valley of Arizona.

The history of Mesa dates to the arrival of the Hohokam people two thousand years ago. The Hohokam tribe built the original canal system in the valley that is still used today. The canals were the largest and most sophisticated in the prehistoric New World, transforming the Sonoran Desert into an agricultural oasis.

After the mysterious disappearance of the Hohokam tribe and before the arrival of the early settlers, explorers did not often travel to the desert area. By the late nineteenth century, U.S. Army troops had relocated the Apache and opened the way for settlements near present-day Mesa.

In March 1877, Mormon pioneers Daniel Webster Jones and Henry Clay Rogers left St. George, Utah, to come south to the Arizona Territory. Jones had been asked by Mormon officials to lead a party of people interested in establishing a new settlement in Arizona. They traveled south and settled on the north side of the current Mesa area. This settlement was initially known as Fort Utah and later as Jonesville. It was located near Lehi Road. In 1883, it was officially named Lehi, as suggested by Brigham Young Jr.

Another group called the First Mesa Company arrived from Utah and Idaho around the same time. Their leaders were Francis Martin Pomeroy, Charles Crismon, George Warren Sirrine and Charels I. Robson. They

Above: Mesa is along the thirty-third parallel (33.4152). *Author's collection.*

Left: Mesa's Main Street, postcard. *Author's collection.*

moved their new settlement onto the mesa that serves as the city's namesake today. They dug irrigation canals using some of those original Hohokam canals to spark their future quest to build successful farms and ranches. Water was flowing through the canals by 1878. The Second Mesa Company arrived in 1879 and settled to the west of the First Mesa Company because there was more available farmland there. This settlement was originally called Alma and later Stringtown. It was located near Alma School Road.

Mesa City was registered as a one-square-mile townsite on July 17, 1878. Its first school was built in 1879. In 1883, Mesa City was incorporated with a population of three hundred. Dr. A.J. Chandler, who would later go on to found the city of Chandler, worked on widening the Mesa Canal in 1895 to allow the flow of water to eventually build a power plant. During the Great Depression, WPA funds aided in paving streets and building a hospital, a new town hall and a library.

With the development of Falcon Field and Williams Field in the early 1940s, more military families began moving into the Mesa area. Air conditioning helped increase tourism, and soon, the population began exploding in the Mesa area.

So, why would Mesa become a hot spot for ghosts? Like the other towns of the Tri-Cities area, Mesa was founded with strong spiritual Native beliefs and the fear one might dishonor a Mormon (or other religious) founder. Perhaps it is just the mixture of so many cultural and ethnic groups settling in one area, bringing in their beliefs and traditions. Or could it be the proximity and power of the mysterious Superstition Mountains to the east of town—or perhaps all the above.

ABANDONED WILLIAMS AFB
6001 SOUTH POWER ROAD
MESA, AZ 85212

Williams Air Force Base, now known as Phoenix-Mesa Gateway Airport, sat on about four thousand acres of land in an area just south of Mesa. The base was established on July 16, 1941, and used for training fighter pilots during World War II. It was named after First Lieutenant Charles Linton Williams, a native of Arizona and a pilot in the U.S. Army Air Corps. Over 26,500 men and women passed through the base and earned their wings there. Williams Air Force Base can boast having the most student pilots graduate from its facility.

In 1993, Williams Air Force Base closed, causing many to lose their jobs and a loss of millions of dollars in annual profits. Plans were eventually redrawn to turn the base into a useable space. It is now a busy airport where hundreds of travelers fly to various destinations each day.

One of the buildings located on the far west side of the base was used as a hospital. Today, it is the local Veterans' Affairs hospital, and there are reports of it being haunted. There have been several sightings of a male ghost in the area once used for viewing newborns. This male ghost has also been seen wandering around the old operating rooms.

And it's just not the old hospital that is haunted. Some employees have said that while they have been in the old officers' club, they have heard disembodied voices. This would have been the gathering place for the officers during World War II. Witnesses have heard footsteps and seen airmen in uniform on the grounds.

Other eyewitnesses have experienced strange things in what was once the old barracks and military housing area. Cadets lived in two different houses on campus while attending school there and had paranormal experiences in both houses. The most activity occurred on a cul-de-sac in the most southwestern neighborhood of the base. Almost everyone who lived on Volante Circle experienced activity in their homes. They saw apparitions, heard noises and even saw a young, ghostly girl walking across the cul-de-sac late at night. There was one experience in which, every time a resident tried to get off the bed, something would growl at them. They never did see anything to explain the mysterious noise.

Another former resident said, "The first strange event that happened was noises in the house. We could hear cabinets and drawers in the kitchen open and close when nobody was in there. It escalated to objects moving in the house. Once, three of us watched as one of those decorated pens with a fluffy feather on top came flying across the room then smacked against the wall, slowly sliding down the wall's surface."

Another time, a resident was in bed, about to fall asleep, when he felt like something was watching from the closet. He stared at it across the dark room, and then, to his horror, the closet door abruptly slid open! It was a metal door on a track. It opened so fast that he thought someone was about to jump out of the closet. The man was paralyzed with fear and let

Williams Army Airfield's main gate. *Courtesy of Wikimedia.*

out a scream. He looked in the closet and saw nothing. No one was there. "Nobody believed me when I said the door had opened on its own," he said.

Others would often see what looked like a man in a long trench coat and rain hat standing inside the abandoned grocery store and sometimes on a street corner late at night. The most terrifying experience occurred one night when a brother and sister were home alone. They both went to sleep before their mother made it home. The brother always slept with his radio on low. A loud noise startled him out of a dead sleep, and he noticed the door to his room had opened, as had the closet door. Before he realized what was going on, a piñata that had been tucked under his bed came out flying at him like someone had thrown it. He jumped out of bed and realized that his closet door was closed, and his radio was turned off. He freaked out! He ran into his sister in the hallway. She said she had heard voices in her room after something had startled her awake. Meanwhile, their mother had been trying to get into the house for more than ten minutes, but the doors would not open. She was about to crawl into a window when, suddenly, the door opened on its own. She thought it was one of the children and was very confused. Twenty years later, the young man still gets goosebumps thinking about that military home.

One eyewitness said,

> *Inside the old hospital, which is now an elementary school, they had the building split into four phases. I was there for all the phases being built except phase 4, which, to this day, has never been completed. Phase 4, from what I can tell, was the area for the mentally ill. I have been through every bit of phase 4, thanks to doing color guard as ASY prepend. I have seen things that are not explainable, and I don't know how to describe them, but no one goes in there alone. One time, I was sent in there alone, which is why no one goes in there alone anymore, because I heard a little girl laughing as well as running down the hallway. I obviously didn't investigate because I was only twelve years old and alone, but I know there was no one else because everyone was in phase 1, the farthest from phase 4. The next day, I went back with a few friends, and when we went toward where I heard the running and laughing, there was a room that looked like it was painted for a little girl. I also heard someone say something about seeing a little girl and boy go into the girls' restroom, but no one ever came out. These were most likely the bathrooms next to the door leading to phase 4, as there have been many sightings at those bathrooms, and those kids are mostly likely the ones I heard—or at least the little girl.*

Some nearby residents say they can hear the phantom sound of the old aircraft engines waiting for takeoff. Are the spirits of air force pilots forever in a holding pattern over the barracks they once called home?

MESA HISTORICAL MUSEUM, OLD LEHI SCHOOL
2345 NORTH HORNE STREET
MESA, AZ 85293

The Mesa Historical Museum (formerly Lehi School) was built on land that was donated to early Lehi settlers by the Rogers family in the 1880s. The school was merely a one-room adobe structure. The community outgrew the small school by the early 1910s, and a new building was needed. The current building was constructed in 1913 and was later expanded in the 1920s. It is the oldest standing school building in the Mesa area. It is known for its modern, Mission/Spanish Revival architectural style. Lehi is now a distinct community within Mesa, Arizona, although Lehi existed prior to the founding of Mesa. Lehi was annexed into its much larger former neighbor in 1970, and it is now the northern limit of central Mesa. Lehi is adjacent to the Salt River on the north and the Consolidated Canal to the south.

During the Great Depression of the 1930s, the Works Progress Administration (WPA) made additional improvements, including a Lehi School auditorium and annex building. The auditorium was so well constructed that it was designated as the community bomb shelter during the Cold War. Later, when the building was no longer needed, due to its sturdy construction, it would have been too costly to tear it down. For this reason, the school and auditorium remain intact and are popular sites for local visitors. The school was placed in the National Register of Historic Places in August 2001.

After getting an early start in the 1940s, the Mesa Historical Museum was incorporated in 1966 by a group of citizens concerned about preserving Mesa's rich history. The museum is dedicated to the preservation of regional heritage. It operates out of the old Lehi School building.

Even with renovations and improvements over the years, the building was finally condemned by the Mesa School District in 1976. The City of Mesa purchased the building and resold it to the Mesa Historic Museum in 1986.

Mesa Historical Museum's main entrance. *Author's collection.*

Mesa Historical Museum's auditorium. *Author's collection.*

The museum opened in 1987 and strives to tell the history of Mesa and the surrounding valley.

In past years, guests have been encouraged to participate in a ghost tour of the old Lehi School in the early evenings during the Halloween season. Led by local paranormal teams, the ghost hunters were instructed to bring their flashlights and cameras to tour the Mesa Historical Museum complex in the spooky, dark afterhours.

One of the museum's buildings that was explored was the auditorium of the former Lehi School, thought to be one of the most haunted locations on the property. Visitors and museum workers have reported seeing a spectral man, thought to be the caretaker of the former school. The ghostly tale states that he died of natural causes in the projector room of the auditorium sometime in the 1970s according to docent Lisa Anderson. While exploring this location and its mysterious tales, one will soon discovery entirely new lessons appreciating historic Mesa.

MESA GRANDE RUINS
1000 NORTH DATE STREET
(CORNER OF DATE AND TENTH STREETS)
MESA, AZ 85201

Mesa Grande Cultural Park in central Mesa preserves a group of Hohokam structures that were constructed during the Classical period. These ruins were occupied between 1100 BCE and 1400 BCE and were products of the Hohokam civilization that inhabited the Salt River Valley. This is where the Hohokam constructed an extensive system of water canals. It is one of only two Hohokam mounds remaining in the metro Phoenix area, the other being the S'eday Va'aki Museum (formerly the Pueblo Grande Museum). The site's central feature is a massive ruin of adobe walls and platforms. The mound was the public and ceremonial center for one of the largest Hohokam villages in the Salt River Valley. It extended for over one mile along the terrace overlooking the river.

It was listed in the National Register of Historic Places in 1978, when it was owned by movie actress Acquanetta and her husband, Jack Ross, who had purchased the site in 1962 from earlier developers. The site was acquired from the couple in 1988 by the City of Mesa. Since the

Take a walk among
the Hohokam ruins.
Author's collection.

2013 completion of the Mesa Grande Visitors Center, the site has been seasonally open to the public from October through May.

The Mesa Grande Cultural Park is operated by the Arizona Museum of Natural History, which is undertaking ongoing archaeological studies there. The mound remains remarkably intact. The general site is protected but undeveloped. The ruins are located to the west and across the street from the former Mesa Lutheran Hospital, which became a Banner Health corporate center that houses billing and information employees.

The Hohokam people constructed the Mesa Grande temple mound. With walls made from *caliche* (the calcium carbonate hardpan that forms under our desert soils), the mound is longer and wider than a modern football field and is twenty-seven feet high. There is an eerie mystery surrounding the abrupt disappearance of the Hohokam civilization. Where did they go? Why did they leave everything behind?

The Lewis family of Mesa, around the turn of the twentieth century, excavated the area known as the Shooting Gallery. The family uncovered the doorway of a room that stood on the mound at an earlier stage of development, when the mound was smaller. One Sunday, they tunneled into the mound, and after digging all morning, they leaned the shovel against the wall of the tunnel and went home to eat lunch. Upon their return, they found that the tunnel had collapsed and buried the shovel inside. Omar Turney, who published this story in 1929, said that archaeologists in the future would be very puzzled when they found the metal shovel buried in a Hohokam mound. The museum's Southwest Archaeology Team recovered the shovel; its wooden handle was intact, but its metal was rusting and disintegrating.

After the Lewis family uncovered these massive, prehistoric walls, they were used as a backstop for a shooting range, giving rise to the name Shooting Gallery. Hundreds of old bullets were recovered here.

Visitors will find a large adobe wall enclosing the mound and a large plaza at the front of it. Volunteers from the Arizona Museum of Natural History constructed a replica of a Hohokam ball court, an open-air structure where ballgames were played using a rubber ball made from a local plant. The ball court is a structure that was important to Hohokam culture. The exact purpose of these courts has been a debate among archaeologists. Some believe they were used for sporting events. Other research suggests they showcased ceremonial traditions or had religious significance.

The Mesa Grande Ruins are adorned with petroglyphs, or carvings into the rock that served as a form of communication, that served as a

An early expedition of the Mesa Hohokam ruins. *Author's collection.*

newspaper for the Hohokam people. These petroglyphs show various patterns of animals and human figures found in their daily lives.

The Mesa Grande Ruins can be found in a quiet neighborhood in the center of Mesa. Some have said it is "a silent testament to the ancient inhabitants of the region." The ancient Hohokam village site is a mysterious window into the past, a portal (or doorway) to a time when the desert was home to thriving communities.

Artifacts presumably associated with the ruins have been found in the neighborhood to the west. Axe heads, arrow heads and pottery sherds were regularly uncovered and collected from just under the surface by residents during the 1960s and 1970s. Residents in neighboring homes and apartment complexes have reported visits from spirits for many years. The MVD Ghostchasers conducted one of their first residential investigations just a block or two from the ruins. Residents reported seeing shadow people moving about their apartments. Although the spirits never caused any harm or danger, it was still alarming to the young families. Once the apartment dwellers were aware of the nearby ruins, a sense of peace settled.

Exploring the Mesa Grande Ruins is not just a visit to an archaeological site; it is also a journey through time. It is a chance to connect with the deep history of the region, to ponder the lives of those who came before

Hohokam ruins. *Author's collection.*

and to appreciate the enduring legacy of the Hohokam people. Many schoolchildren drive past the site with their parents without knowing the history. Debe Branning remembers taking her daughter to the fenced area in the early 1990s. "We stopped and photographed the area late one evening. My daughter did not feel comfortable. She sensed that someone was watching us."

The Mesa Grande Ruins are more than just a cultural, historical treasure. It is a spiritual location where the past speaks to the present. Walk among the preserved ancient structures and admire the petroglyphs. Think about the mysteries of the Hohokam people. You will soon be transported to a time and place of long, long ago. Remember, this land in Mesa was once the home of a thriving and vibrant civilization. It's a wonderful place to meditate and reflect on the enduring connection between humans and the land. The reminders of the past are what carry us into today's world.

The Mesa Grande Ruins silently sit proudly in a quiet, suburban neighborhood. Even today, many people do not know the village is there. But the neighbors say you can still hear the whispers in the night. Are these the undertones of the mysterious Hohokam people—or their spirits communicating in the wind?

A STROLL THROUGH MESA CITY CEMETERY
1212 NORTH CENTER STREET
MESA, AZ 85213

The City of Mesa Cemetery was first established in 1883, following a smallpox epidemic that claimed the lives of forty-four residents of the small community. As Mesa's population began to grow, more space was needed for the dearly departed. In 1891, land was purchased along Center Street, just north of Brown Road, for this purpose.

Part of the original Mesa Cemetery was located on the land where the Circle K at the corner of University and Center Streets now stands. Clerks at the Circle K have noticed paranormal activity inside the convenience store from time to time. The graves of these early pioneers were moved to the historical section of the current Mesa Cemetery. Just north of the cemetery office is a section dedicated to "those persons unknown buried during the Great Depression." These folks were interred during a bleak period, when permanent memorials were often a luxury.

Once a year, informative guides from the Mesa Historical Society lead a cemetery tour through the older section of the cemetery, which takes guests to the final resting places of many of the pioneer families who have made an impact on Mesa, creating the leading community it is today.

Mesa City Cemetery is the final resting place of Mesa's four founding fathers: Charles Crismon, Frances Pomeroy, Charles Robson and George W. Sirrine. Nearby is the grave site of Daniel Webster Jones, who founded the neighboring town of Lehi. His grandson Daniel D. Jones was the first child born in Lehi.

An airbase was used in Mesa during World War II for the training of United States and British fighter pilots. Over two thousand men were trained at Falcon Field, which today serves as Mesa's municipal airport. During the years the airfield served as a training facility, twenty-three British cadets and one American pilot were killed in air accidents there. These individuals were buried in a special section of the Mesa Cemetery.

Other notable people who are buried there include country singer-songwriter Waylon Jennings (1937–2002), the popular country western superstar with over sixty albums and sixteen number-one country singles. The Texas musician became extremely popular while living in Arizona, so it was only fitting he was buried there. Visitors often leave shots of tequila on his grave marker.

This page, top: Mesa Cemetery's gate is inviting. *Author's collection.*

This page, bottom: The grave marker of Waylon Jennings at Mesa Cemetery. *Author's collection.*

Opposite: The Mesa Cemetery grave marker of Mesa High School football player Zedo Ishikawa. *Author's collection.*

廣島縣廣島市古田町

石川次郎墓

大正五年五月三十日生
昭和七年九月二十二日殁

ZEDO ISHIKAWA
BORN IN M....AY 31, 1915
DIED IN M........22, 1932

William A. Burton, who operated Mesa's first mortuary, was also buried in the Mesa Cemetery. And on the other end of the spectrum, you can find the grave site of nurse Helen Dana, who operated a maternity home, took in unwed mothers and delivered over 12,500 babies in the Mesa area. Dr. Lucius C. Alston (1892–1958) was Mesa's first Black physician and was known to treat anyone who needed care, regardless of race or ability to pay.

There is a bittersweet stop at the tombstone of Zedo Ishikawa (1915–1932), a young athlete who played on the Mesa High School football team. His last wish of "Carry On" continues to be the high school's motto. Zedo died following an accident on his family's farm near Mesa. He was very popular and was the football team's starting quarterback.

Stop at the marker of John L. Lee and his wife, Kitty. John was an entertainer and former member of *Buffalo Bill Cody's Wild West Show–Powder River*. John L. Lee popularized the American folk song "Red River Valley."

Another popular tombstone in the cemetery is that of Ernesto Miranda (1941–1976), whose 1966 Supreme Court case resulted in the establishment of the Miranda warning.

In the past, the cemetery tour visited the military grave of Confederate soldier Martin Van Worthington. He was buried in the cemetery in an unmarked grave for ninety-seven years. Funds were raised, and he now has a stone to honor his service.

And do not forget the area's early business proprietors, such as the Goodmans, who operated Apache Drugs; Orley Stapley, who ran the hardware store that sent supplies up to the construction workers at the Roosevelt Dam; and John Riggs, who ran his early blacksmith shop.

Now, the pioneers all lie side by side in a city of the dead under the protection of cypress trees in the historic portion of the Mesa City Cemetery. There are many trees in the cemetery, and the landscape offers a park-like setting for a comfortable stroll through Mesa's history.

Longtime residents will recall when the cemetery was the place for local teens to hunt for ghosts back in the days when the tall gates to the cemetery were left unlocked and unattended after dark. These ghost hunters never knew what they were going to encounter during their late-night games of hide-and-seek! MVD Ghostchaser Cindy recalled a story her late mother once told her. A group of high school girls had ventured into the cemetery one evening on a dare. All was going well until one of the girls saw a shadowy figure, which sent the ladies running toward the front gate. The jacket of one of the teens became entangled on a bush, and her instinct told her something or someone had grabbed her. She screamed and collapsed to

Above: Ernesto Miranda rests at Mesa Cemetery. *Courtesy of Pinterest.*

Right: The bread box mausoleum at Mesa Cemetery. *Author's collection.*

the ground. The paramedics were called, and she was rushed to the local hospital. The girl, who apparently had a bad heart, later died. You could say she was frightened to death!

The cemetery's tall, shadowy trees, or "spook trees," as the youngsters like to call them, will hold the tales of history and mysteries of the old settlers for all eternity.

INSIDE THE BUNGALOW
48 NORTH ROBSON STREET
MESA, AZ 85201

Folks in Mesa enjoy a relaxing spot of tea or tasty cup of coffee at Inside the Bungalow, which has been located, for several years, in downtown Mesa's original town square. This was once the home of a prominent Mesa doctor, Eli C. Openshaw. The Openshaw family moved into the bungalow-style home in the early 1910s. This turn-of-the-century house is tucked away behind beautiful flowers and plant life and gives you the feeling of visiting your great-aunt's home on a Sunday afternoon. The coffeehouse has offered yoga classes, workshops and even a romantic setting for county garden weddings. It is also a location where a tea party might run into a ghost from the past. The historic bungalow, with its famous twisty-turvy brick chimney, stands quietly near First and Robson Streets.

It is thought that many of the sprits of the Openshaw family, the home's residents from early 1910s to the mid-1950s, still visit their former home. There were reports of ghostly activity soon after the house was converted into a quaint, busy little coffee shop known as Coffee Talk in the late 1990s and early 2000s.

Many patrons have seen an elderly gentleman strolling from room to room or out in the back gardens of the bungalow. The owners told this author of an incident in which a customer was started by the appearance of a woman in the ladies' restroom.

Heather Rhyneer of East Valley Paranormal stated she once ventured upstairs, where the owners used to sell lovely period clothing. She looked up from the item she had been admiring and noticed an older woman staring at her. She asked the woman a question and was ignored. Feeling the lady was being quite rude, Michelle went back downstairs to get more

Inside the bungalow in Mesa. *Author's collection.*

information from the owner. She told the owner what had happened near the clothing area and said that she felt put off by the woman upstairs. The owner just smiled and explained there was no salesperson upstairs. Heather had seen the ghost.

Medora Openshaw is said to have died in the home in October 1957 of a heart ailment. She was seventy-nine years old. Could this have been the ghostly woman who was seen near the ladies' restroom and the upstairs sales display?

It has also been noted that a ghostly young girl has been seen playing in the gardens of the backyard. The Openshaws welcomed several children into their home. The door was always open to their many nieces and nephews who lived in the same Mesa neighborhood.

One of the ghosts is thought to be the spirit of the Openshaws' young son Noah G. Openshaw. Noah tragically drowned in the Salt River at the Roosevelt Dam during a family outing in March 1914. The ten-year-old lad stepped into the rushing waters and was suddenly overpowered by the whirling torrents of water. The funeral was held at the Openshaw family home on Robson Street. Many family members and friends came to pay their respects.

Another visitor had been attending the annual Mesa Historic Home Tours when she discovered the energies of Inside the Bungalow. Being a bit of an empath, she described how the spirits suddenly became busy during her stop on the tour.

She recalled,

While walking through the house with a friend of mine, it felt like I was walking through a crowd and that every table and chair was occupied. The actual place was only at 40 percent capacity, even with the flow of visitors coming and going on the self-guided tour. The impression of laughter and conservation, however, felt like there was a larger gathering going on—full of friends. It felt like a gathering place for the living and the dead. It was much easier to breathe outside in the courtyard. I hadn't looked up at the roof the building, but one of the tour guides stationed at the bungalow pointed out the custom-built chimney. This seemed to be a focal point of the spiritual energy—giving off energy like some sort of a beacon. It was built of brick in a unique spiral pattern, topped with an onion shaped vent cam. As I looked at it, it was as though the lines of energy fed up the sides of the chimney and dispersed in every direction.

The owners of Inside the Bungalow have always confirmed the spirits inside the historic building are friendly and have caused no harm to any of their frequent patrons. Gather your friends and enjoy a quiet afternoon tea or relaxing evening on the patio. The ghostly spirits are simply that extra shot of cream in your coffee—if you are one of those who like a little spirit in your coffee or perhaps a spot of supernatural in your tea.

THE BOY IN THE ATTIC

The home on Wilbur Street is a private residence, but feel free to visit Ross at Mesa City Cemetery.

Always on the prowl for a haunting or ghost investigation, this author decided to take the Walking Tour of Mesa's Historical Homes. There is a theory that renovating buildings sometimes stirs up spirits and paranormal activity, so I carefully tucked my digital camera and EMF meter in my backpack and began my quest for a good ghost story.

As I approached the small adobe house on Wilbur Street, my eyes were immediately attracted to a small window in the attic. It gave me a sad, distant feeling. My attention focused on the homeowner, Janice, who was standing at the top of the steps. A tall, statuesque woman, she was telling the story and the background history of her recently renovated home to a tour group. She seemed to know every brick and board in the structure. I learned she had done most of the labor on the house herself, camping out in the home with no running water or electricity for two years as she worked. She became a part of the house, just as the one-hundred-year-old structure became a part of her. She let the small group in to tour the home while I stayed behind to speak to her.

"Excuse me," I inquired, "Did you, by chance, notice any paranormal activity while you renovated the house?"

Her eyes widened, and a smile came across her face. She pointed to a chair and asked me to have a seat.

"Funny you should ask," she said with enthusiasm. "I have had psychics come here because I had heard knocking in the attic. I work at the Mesa Library, and during my research on the house, I learned a young boy named Ross, aged twelve, died in the attic during a flu epidemic back in 1918. People in those days often quarantined the sick from the rest of the family, and Ross apparently spent what little of his life remained tucked away in the attic. His mother served him food and drink through a hole in the attic floor. Perhaps he knocked whenever he needed her attention. The psychics claim they have cleared the house, and so far, things have been okay."

I handed her my card. "If anything ever changes, please call me." I walked away, sneaking another glance at the attic window. Was that a shadow of a boy I saw staring down at the touring groups below?

Two months later, I received a frantic call from Janice, the homeowner. It seemed that the activity had begun again, and this time, it was even more intense! The knocking had resumed, keys were turning up missing and there was loud stomping in the dining area. One evening, I brought a small paranormal investigation team to her house. We asked her to tell us the story of Ross and the house so we could analyze the mystery of the restless young spirit and put things in perspective.

The historic adobe home originally sat on West First Street, facing the south. It was in that location that the boy and his family resided in the home. In 1995, the City of Mesa ordered the house to be torn down to make space for a parking lot. Janice rescued it from demolition and moved it to its present location, where it now faces the east.

"I feel Ross is confused," I told Janice. "He looks out the window and does not understand why the view is different. That is why he paces. He does not realize the house has been moved."

"It is not the only time he has been moved," Janice explained. "The old Mesa Cemetery was first located at Center Street and University Drive. Ross's grave was later moved to a new burial site at the present Mesa Cemetery."

As we spoke of Ross, we could hear movement from the attic, and the lights over the dining room table flickered. The team took several photographs with digital cameras. We decided to set up the night camera and digital recorders in the attic overnight. We could almost feel Ross watching us as we set the equipment up in the small, hot attic space. On our way down the narrow attic steps, the light switch physically turned itself off.

The next day, I retrieved our equipment and began analyzing the data. No images were recorded, but there was the sound of soft shuffling about the room. At some point, Ross's curiosity got the best of him. A clapping sound could be clearly heard, as if he was trying to test and understand the function of the camera and recording devices. During the taping, the date suddenly appeared and disappeared on the screen, as if Ross had tried touching the buttons on the camera.

Janice called me the next day. "I don't know what you did upstairs, but we could hear Ross pacing the attic all night! I think it is time to let him go. I have been talking to him for seven years as if he was my own son. He must think of me as his mother. This is not fair to either one of us. It will be hard, but it is time for him to move on and go to the light."

I agreed. A week later, I brought in Mark Christoph, a paranormal investigator, and a medium named Trisha Dolan to aid Ross in his journey to the beyond. We headed for the hot attic, where we planned to persuade Ross it was time to move on to the light and be with his dear mother again. Trisha smudged the room with sage for our protection. We formed a circle on the attic floor, lit a white candle and began our work. Trisha led us in a meditation, asking for a white light of love, protection and healing power to surround us. She began speaking to Ross and told him there was no need to stay earthbound.

Ross's mother died of the same illness as Ross one week after her son's death. Aware of his mother's illness, Ross remained earthbound to watch over her in case she should pass on. Unfortunately, Ross's mother thought her son had gone to heaven after he died. When she passed on, she went directly into the light and was gone. Poor Ross was left behind. They buried the bodies of Ross and his mother together, and soon, life resumed in the house. Being a young boy, Ross had no idea what to do. He was waiting for his mother to return and take him to heaven. He waited a long, long time. Then Janice showed up as the new owner of the house. Childless, Janice eventually took on the ghost child as her own.

That night in the attic, we could sense the fear that gripped Ross. He was afraid we would remove him from the house before his mother could return for him. He feared he would never see her again. Trisha continued to reassure Ross that we were there to help him. We all felt a deep sadness in the room.

Suddenly, Ross began to conduit through Janice. His heavy weeping filled the room!

"I don't want to go!" Ross sobbed through Janice's trembling voice. "I can't breathe. My chest and my throat hurt so bad!"

"It is from the flu," Trisha tried to calm him. "Let yourself go toward the light, and you will not feel any more pain. Look into the light, Ross!"

"I can't see it!" Ross cried as Janice squeezed her eyes shut. He was still resisting.

"Open your eyes, Ross, and look into the candlelight." Trisha urged. "Your mother is there waiting for you with outstretched arms!"

"I am feeling lighter," Ross declared, again speaking through Janice. Trisha and I both reached over and placed one hand on Janice's knees to keep her grounded and earthbound. "I feel like I am flying!"

"That's good, Ross," Trisha encouraged him. "Keep following the light!"

"I am flying over the rooftops," Ross said in awe. "I am high above the trees!"

Ross's energy disappeared, and the room returned to normal. It was calmer, cooler, and a sense of peace filled the attic. "It's OK. It's me now," Janice said in her own voice. We gave her a hug and thanked her for being there for Ross as he made his transition.

We all went downstairs, and the entire house seemed brighter, like it carried a lighter atmosphere. Janice thanked us and promised to keep us informed of any follow-up activity. We left the house, and for the first time, it felt peaceful again.

When I viewed the video filmed during our last visit with Ross, it clearly showed us in the attic, sitting in our circle. Ross could be heard speaking through Janice in a frightened voice. Mysteriously, the tape became cloudy and fuzzy as Ross spoke of flying to heaven. As soon as Janice was grounded, the picture became clear and focused again.

The next afternoon, I went to the Mesa Cemetery and located the grave of Ross and his mother. I was overcome with a sense of happiness and peace,

The grave of the boy in the attic in Mesa Cemetery. *Author's collection.*

for Ross had been reunited with his mother and all was well. I left a bouquet of flowers on their grave. Janice had left him an orange.

There has been no further activity at the adobe house on Wilbur Street since that June evening. The boy in the attic is free at last!

THE LANDMARK RESTAURANT
(NOW KNOWN AS THE LANDMARK WEDDING VENUE)
809 WEST MAIN STREET
MESA, AZ 85201

The former Landmark Restaurant's gabled roof building was once the home of a Mormon church built back in 1908. An open canal on the east side of the church nourished large cottonwood trees along its banks that provided shade for gatherings. The church was housed in what was the main dining room of the Landmark. The front door faced north onto Main Street. The Sunday school rooms were located downstairs. In 1939, the church underwent some extensive remodeling procedures, which updated the building to look much like it does today.

Two buildings south of the restaurant were later added and used for social events. The larger building, Heritage Hall, was built for recreational purposes for the church in the late 1920s. The smaller building behind the patio was built in the 1930s to be used as a Boy Scouts meeting room. The congregation grew large in the 1950s, so the church moved to other quarters in the Mesa area. The building was used to house the offices of an insurance company, and later, it was the original site of the Mesa Community College campus.

The first restaurant to occupy the building was opened in 1972 and was rightly named Rouch's Schoolhouse Restaurant. Then on New Year's Day 1981, the Ellises, who had recently moved to Arizona, opened the Landmark Restaurant. The restaurant had several banquet rooms available for luncheons, company dinners and special events with friends and family. The upstairs dining room attracted guests for evenings of intimate dining. Each of the salad room's menu selections were renowned for being delicious and filling meals.

The MVD Ghostchasers offered a paranormal workshop at the Landmark Restaurant in January 2005. The paranormal team was joined by twenty-eight attendees who were curious to learn more about the Landmark and its ghosts. They gathered in one of the spacious banquet rooms in the lower level of the restaurant. The restaurant closed sharply at 9:00 p.m. The ghost investigators then had access to the entire building as the staff quietly prepared the Landmark for the following day's business.

Breaking into smaller groups, the investigators explored various rooms throughout the facility. Some of the folks went upstairs to photograph the main dining room, the clock room and upper stairway. Others remained downstairs to check out the kitchen, the Victorian room and the bottom staircase, where some patrons had felt a cool breeze passing them on the lower step. A smaller group went directly to the ladies' room, where a woman's presence had been sensed. Some guests and staff often noted water faucets mysteriously turning on and off in the restroom.

A staff member had a set of keys to the large Heritage Hall and offered to let the group in to do further investigation. Almost everyone joined together in the adjacent building to explore the hall and its basement. Many people photographed orbs on and around the stage. While everyone was filming in the hall, a couple of the many psychics participating in the workshop were sent on a walk through the restaurant portion of the old church.

MVD Ghostchasers team member Mark Christoph found a dark corner in the basement of Heritage Hall to sit in and communicate with the spirits.

The former Landmark Restaurant was once a church. *Wikimedia Commons.*

Mark sat alone in the confinement of the lonely basement for almost an hour. He filmed the depressing area with his night-vision infrared camera. He said whatever was in the dank basement began to affect him adversely. Mark became lightheaded, shaky and sweaty, even though it was a chilly Arizona winter evening. Another MVD Ghostchaser, Chris McCurdy, joined him in the small area. He did not like the feeling he experienced in the tiny basement either and immediately went back upstairs. Almost every paranormal investigator who was brave enough to tour the small, dark basement felt a heavy presence there, a sense of sadness, and not one of them wanted to stay down there very long.

This brings us back to the controversial ghost in the ladies' restroom. The restaurant staff had nicknamed the ghost in the bathroom Bea. Bea had been known to turn the sink faucets on and off. For a moment, the group thought they had their own ghostly encounter with Bea. They quietly entered the restroom with a local news camera crew tailing behind them. To their surprise, the camera crew suddenly discovered the battery power on the boom mic and cameras had been lost! Tamara Jaffe did not sense extreme activity in the ladies' restroom, but she did feel a cold chill and sensed weeping in the room.

As the group photographed the restroom area, the faucets suddenly turned on and off, sending members of the news team running out of the bathroom. Anxiously, the investigators gathered and reviewed the video from the camera. While analyzing the video data, they noticed that the flash of one of the digital cameras triggered the infrared electronic eye sensors on the faucets, as did any exaggerated arm waving near the faucets. Debunked!

The group concluded that if Bea is lurking in the ladies' room, she is not in control of the plumbing.

One of the former busboys shared an interesting ghost tale he witnessed when he was employed at the Landmark.

An older gentleman asked me for directions from the main dining room to the bathroom, which is located downstairs. The elderly man had just been released from the hospital earlier that day after having extensive surgery. Unfortunately, the man took a tumble down the restaurant stairs, but somehow, he had crawled back up to the top of the stairs, where he could seek help. The paramedics were immediately called, and I stood helpless as the EMTs tried valiantly to save him. Sadly, his fall caused internal bleeding, and I watched the man die on the stairs.

A month later, the busboy was back on the job, working his normal shift.

A car accident in the area caused a power failure throughout parts of downtown Mesa, including the Landmark. I was sent downstairs to get candles from the banquet rooms. I placed them on the stairs leading out of the restaurant to offer lighting for the guests. When the restaurant was free of diners, the employees worked quickly to clean the dimly lit rooms of the restaurant. I was later asked to return the candles back downstairs and to reset the tables in the Victorian room.

I cleaned the banquet room with only minimal lighting. While resetting one of the tables near the inside of the doorway, I noticed a gentleman walking down the long hallway. The man was near the door to the garden room and was walking away from me. I tried to get the attention of the gentleman, but the man did not acknowledge me at all! I repeated myself in a much louder, bolder tone. There was no reaction from the elderly man. I thought the gentleman was simply hard of hearing and had returned to retrieve an article he left behind in a dining room. I stepped in front of him and said loudly, "Excuse me, sir, but the restaurant is closed, and you're not allowed down here." The man said nothing and kept on walking. Now, the gentleman turned quickly into the Roosevelt room. I followed behind the man so he could be escorted out of the restaurant safely. I entered the Roosevelt room, only to find it empty. I even kneeled to the floor to try and look under a tablecloth. I bolted back upstairs and told my sister that I could not work there anymore. I later looked back at this experience and wondered if this was the ghostly gentleman who fell down the stairs.

These are some of the reports the guests at this early paranormal workshop provided to Debe Branning. All in all, it was a busy evening, and the spirits interacted with nearly every guest!

Tamara Jaffe, a holistic practitioner, began her walk upstairs on the main floor with MVD Ghostchasers team member Maddie Kinder. Maddie jotted down Tamara's impressions as a crew member from AZCentral.com filmed the psychic medium at work. Tamara felt a strong, heavy energy in the dining room. The Mormon church was originally housed in what was then the main dining room. The restaurant staff often felt off balance when they stood in the area near the waitstaff work center in this dining room. Jaffe believed the room still carried deep emotions from its days as a Mormon church. Later, it was discovered that, in photographs, Chelby Geiss had captured a moving energy orb close to the ground circulating between the chairs and table legs.

James Kelly, a workshop paranormal investigator who specializes in EVP, felt a sharp pain slice into his lower stomach area, and he almost doubled over as he entered the dining room. As he turned to exit, Tamara entered the room. She, too, expressed that something had passed through her and that felt it in her stomach. James found this to be an odd coincidence.

James also reported major equipment failure in the clock room. Two ladies in the room were diligently using dowsing rods to locate spirit activity. As James scanned them with a thermal device, the temperature in the room dropped from 69 degrees Fahrenheit to 60 degrees Fahrenheit within a second as the rods twirled and popped. The temperature returned to 69 degrees Fahrenheit as soon as the presence they detected was gone. Tamara felt an angry male presence as soon as she stepped into the clock room. She sensed many unresolved emotional issues remained behind in the timeless room.

In the downstairs Victorian banquet room, Jaffe felt a young girl was lost in the cabinet closet under the staircase. She sensed the girl was afraid to go into the light. Tamara saw the number 15 and the name Kristin or Ellen.

Yvonne Parkhill, another psychic medium who attended the workshop, also explored the restaurant. This time, MVD Ghostchaser Shiela McCurdy wrote down Yvonne's perceptions of the building. Once again, the camera crew followed closely behind. In the salad room, which was an entire room designated for a huge salad bar, Yvonne felt the hustle and bustle of female energy. Perhaps this was a ladies' meeting room at one time.

Upstairs in the main dining room, Yvonne's focus went to hearing the singing and entertainment that once filled the room. The room also presented an underlying feeling of great sternness. The heavy feeling may have been residual energy brought on by the strict regimen of the Mormon religion from an earlier time. She felt the presence of a man feared by all. He was almost God-like, perhaps the bishop of the church, feared and revered by the congregation.

Yvonne felt there was a sanctuary in the clock room, as though there was no public access and that it was a quiet place used for reflection or meditation. Workshop attendee Lisa McDaniel felt there was a young woman looking out of a window in this room, as though she was waiting for someone to return. This window once faced the original street entrance of the church before it was changed to the current passage on a side street.

Back downstairs, the group revisited the Victorian room. Yvonne again felt the presence of a stern man of judgment. In the crawl space under the stairs, she sensed children afraid of punishment. Lisa McDaniel also sensed a young child very scared in this dark closet.

Nance Card, a psychic investigator, came all the way from Nevada to participate in the evening workshop. In the main dining room, she sensed a young girl's ears being "boxed" by her father, perhaps for not giving the religious service her undivided attention.

The investigators took several group photographs on the main staircase in the hopes that some of the ghostly patrons would join in on a Kodak photo moment. Someone sensed an entity sitting near Mark Christoph's shoulder. However, he did not feel that anyone had become attached to him or followed him home from his time in the basement.

Robin Abels, another workshop regular, sat on a bench at the foot of the lower stairs for quite a spell. She felt a cold chill around her. It seemed to be the energy of a small girl around eight years old. Robin also photographed a nice ectoplasm shot outside the main building as she was leaving for home.

The Landmark Restaurant closed in May 2015 and is now a wedding and reception venue. Is the building still filled with spirits that share a strong emotional attachment to their former church? You may feel in awe when you sit down to revel at the elegant venue. Leave a place setting across the table for any unseen guests and please be reminded to say grace as your evening's celebration begins!

THE WANDERING JEFFERSON PARK GHOST
306 JEFFERSON AVENUE
MESA, AZ 85208

Jefferson Park is located in a Mesa residential neighborhood that offers a ball field and volleyball and basketball courts. It features several picnic table areas and a playground with modern equipment for toddlers and young children. By all accounts, it is a great local family park enjoyed by the community. However, as the daylight wanes and the shadows move in, the park begins to suggest a more sinister reputation that provides some dark, unusual activity that most attribute to a female ghost that is bound in the park forever.

The urban legend behind the ghost of Jefferson Park states that a woman was assaulted and murdered in the park. Although no death certificates or news articles have been uncovered to provide facts and verification to this accusation, many paranormal investigators in the Tri-City area have made the trek in the late-night hours in hopes of recording EVPs (electronic voice phenomena) or capturing the shadowy specter on their cameras.

Jefferson Park's entrance sign. *Author's collection.*

Most legends surrounding the ghost say she is most often spotted between the hours of 11:30 p.m. and midnight and seen moving from tree to tree throughout the park. Visitors to the neighborhood gathering place after nightfall are usually aware of the tales of the Jefferson Park Ghost, and many keep a vigilant (and perhaps almost protective) eye out for her.

Some paranormal investigators have seen a little girl near the swings at the playground equipment. Many have witnessed an empty swing moving back and forth as though a child is at play. During these sightings, there is no breeze, nor are there any other swings in motion.

Costas Gioldasis of Gold Rush Paranormal visited the park late one evening and stood close to the public restrooms. It wasn't long before he

64

Jefferson Park's haunted restroom. *Author's collection.*

saw the shadowy figure of a woman moving near the trees. Using a Ghost Box he heard the words *rape*, *Eva*, *bathroom* and *trapped*. Costas then grabbed an Echobox, from which he heard, "A guy waited in bathroom." Did this paranormal investigator make contact the mysterious specter?

One ghost investigator said,

> *I started dating my wife at the end of August 2007. My favorite holiday is Halloween, so I thought we should do something fun, like go to a party or a zombie walk, but she was scheduled to work until 10:30 p.m. at a local coffee shop. I decided to hang out with some of my friends, and we looked online for some legitimately haunted places in Phoenix. I found a few that sounded cool, and then we ran across one at Jefferson Park in Mesa. We just had to check it out because I had gone to Jefferson Elementary as a kid—the school is located just a bit north of the park.*
>
> *The story of the haunting on the website told of a young girl who had been raped and murdered at the south end of the park near Broadway Road in the early 1990s. I sort of remember hearing about this when I was a kid, but my family lived on the other side of the freeway in a different neighborhood, so they were not very concerned. My wife (girlfriend at the time) and I got to the park around 11:00 p.m. and sat on the swings talking until around 1:30 a.m. I decided the story was total BS and told my wife we should go home. Right then (no kidding, RIGHT THEN), we both saw a female walking along the southwestern edge of the park. There were no streetlights on that end of the park, so she was looking very shadowy. She also seemed to be walking ridiculously fast. It seemed sort of normal, but at the same time, there was something odd about it.*

Finally, we realized that she had no gait! It was like she was gliding or floating very quickly along the sidewalk. Then it became even a little weirder. There are streetlights on the southeastern edge of the park, but when the ghost arrived there, she was still shadowy! She turned north and walked up Jefferson Avenue. We watched her until she was occluded by one of the buildings.

We ran to the car to try and drive past whomever it was we saw—just to make sure it wasn't a worker on their way home. But there was no one walking down Jefferson Avenue. We looked and began to drive up and down each street coming off Jefferson—but still saw no sign of any person walking. It was very WEIRD!

Another frazzled ghost hunter said,

A friend and I read about this park on a website years ago and decided to check out the rumors ourselves. We arrived around 11:30 p.m., and we were both too scared to leave the car—so we just rolled down the windows and waited. Shortly after midnight, we both heard a very loud woman's scream coming from inside the park. We could see that there was no one in or around the park. Normally, I don't believe in this sort of stuff, but I can't deny what we both heard! Super scary!

SUNKIST FACTORY WAREHOUSE
254 WEST BROADWAY ROAD
MESA, AZ 85210

The Mesa Citrus Growers Association operated its busy packinghouse for nearly seventy-five years. The factory officially opened in the 1930s, and the valley growers sold their fruit under the Sunkist brand name. Factory workers packaged and processed citrus fruit at this location, with production peaking in the 1995–96 season. It was the last major packinghouse in Tri-City area. The seventy-thousand-square-foot, orange-brick warehouse sat on a little more than seven acres conveniently next to Mesa's railroad tracks. In its heyday, the factory packed 1.2 million cartons of citrus each season. During the busy packing season, the packinghouse employed 150 to 200 people. As with any produce factory or processing plant, the Sunkist factory had accidents, injuries and, sometimes, deaths.

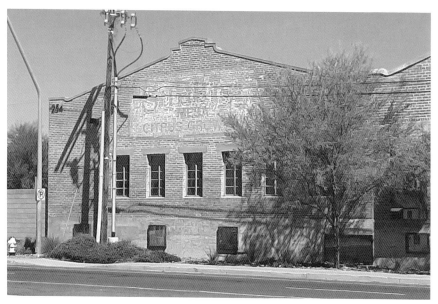

Above: The Sunkist building from a distance. *Author's collection.*

Left: The Sunkist factory. *Courtesy of COPS Crew.*

In 2010, the citrus packing plant closed, and the building remained vacant for several years. Vagrants and the homeless moved into the empty space. Over time, there were several overdoses, suicides and deaths that occurred on the nearby train tracks.

Today, the former citrus packaging plant houses business for brands operating under the parent company Autoline Industries, an innovative manufacturing and distribution business. It has also been used as a wedding and reception venue. It is ideal for photo shoots, car shows and more.

Several Arizona paranormal teams, such as the Cahal Crew and Spiritual Paranormal Investigators of Arizona, have explored the large facility. They recorded voices and whistling and have been touched during investigations.

On a brisk Friday the thirteenth in November 2015, the COPS (Crossing Over Paranormal Society) crew conducted their Sunkist Group Ghost Hunt at the facility. About twenty-five paranormal enthusiasts showed up for an opportunity to participate in a full-scale paranormal investigation alongside the COPS crew.

Debe Branning had the good fortune of being invited by Jay Yates, the founder of the COPS paranormal team, and joined the tour. Yates led the evening tour, telling the history of the building and explaining some of the equipment the group would be using during the investigation. Over the years, his paranormal team investigated the empty halls of the factory, and they were anxious to share some of their discoveries and data. The walking tour guests were able to explore the main floor, basement and offices of the landmark building. The COPS crew shared reports of shadow people, unexplained sounds, light touches and responses on the Ovilus and RemPod devices they detected in the past. Jay encountered the spirit of a woman in the building on several occasions. Is she the woman who was killed on the tracks by a freight train that was passing on the north side of the Sunkist factory?

Construction workers at the site have seen someone peeking at them from around the corner and a ball mysteriously moving from location to another in the large facility. The energies have also often played pranks on

The Sunkist factory, opened in the 1930s. *Author's collection.*

them. There seemed to be areas of cold spots in the basement that could not be explained.

The investigators—some experienced and some new in the field—spent four hours, from 8:00 p.m. until midnight, in the old manufacturing plant. They traveled about the old factory that had, until recently, not been explored by any paranormal investigative team.

The guest investigators reported seeing shadow people, hearing unexplained sounds and making contact with the unknown using various detection devices. Some of their equipment was picking up messages in Spanish. In the factory's early days, many migrant workers made up its working force. One group felt cold spots in unlikely locations in the basement, and one gentleman saw a male shadow out of the corner of his eye. Some of the groups utilized the flashlight test—asking yes or no questions and waiting for the light to blink on and off in response. The batteries in the team members' cameras and equipment drained inexplicably, while EMF readings were sky high.

Jay Yates added, "Toward the end of the night, we found ourselves chasing what appeared to be disembodied voices in the basement and encountered several bizarre temperature changes in the process."

All the participating investigators enjoyed the chance to ghost hunt with their peers under the supervision of a team who could show them the ropes. For many of the guests, it was their first encounter with the unknown. Would they do it again?

"Yes!" One guest smiled. "This was my first investigation. Now, I am hooked!"

Orange you glad the spirits remained at the factory and did not get canned?

MESA'S MYSTERIOUS TUNNELS AND TOURS
RYDABLES
WWW.RYDABLES.COM

Over the years, in the weeks preceding Halloween, the darkened streets of Mesa have become eerie venues with groups of ghost seekers taking the Mesa Ghost Tour. Members of the Mesa Historical Society and Mesa Convention and Visitors' Bureau escorted guests on a quest for the paranormal on the annual Mesa Ghost Tour and Historical Walk. The walking tour combined a bit of history of Mesa's downtown city center with eerie tales of ghosts and possible haunted historic buildings. With the flick of a cape, tour groups are led down the spooky streets.

The tour made several stops along Main Street, where the ghost hunting guests heard firsthand accounts of paranormal activity from Mesa business owners. They made visits to some of Mesa's oldest buildings and learned their histories and why the present-day ghostly visitations still occur. Many of these old buildings still retain their 1900 features, such as original brick walls and raised tin ceilings.

Members of the paranormal teams Arizona Paranormal Investigations, Phoenix Arizona Paranormal Society and Ghosts of Arizona were on hand to talk about their experiences and to demonstrate equipment and EVP techniques.

The tour groups visited Sun Dust Gallery and headed downstairs to the mysterious underground tunnels that were constructed under the buildings and streets of Mesa. Some say these tunnels were used for storage, ventilation or perhaps to hide a bit of bootlegging during Prohibition. The gallery owner reported once going down into the basement area to find panes of shelving glass that had been neatly stacked in a tall pile scattered across the basement floor. None of the sheets of glass had been broken.

Early Mesa Main Street. *Courtesy of Mesa History Museum.*

Old Hotel Sanatorium in downtown Mesa. *Author's collection.*

The dining area of Sweet Cakes Café was once a small travel agency run by a single agent. Once, she said she could not find her keys anywhere. After an extensive search, she found them in the building adjacent to her rear wall. She had not been in the other building that day. The bakers at Sweet Cakes Café have noted strange things happening in the wee hours of the night, when they are hard at work baking up delicious goodies for the next day. One of the bakers was frightened one evening when she witnessed a beautiful woman's face hovering high up in the corner of the shop. The baker could see the woman's face and eyes clearly and at first believed it was a portrait hanging on the wall in the darkened room. The next day, the baker realized there was no picture of a woman on the wall and decided to make the ghostly image her friend. The baker has also heard voices and old-fashioned music. She turned her own radio volume on high to override the noises.

The Drew building, constructed in 1912, was the location of a grocery store and furniture store. The upscale Drew Apartments on the second floor seem to have captured a lot of residual energy within their brick walls. Several apartment residents have seen water faucets turn on and off and thermostats go haywire. They have also heard the noises of someone walking around in the hallways and have had complaints from neighbors about wild, loud parties when there are no parties at all. One tenant said her cat has been sensitive to something in the building. Her radio has been known to turn on by itself and suddenly blare loudly, disturbing the other tenants. The renters believe that the friendly ghosts of Edith and Rose reside in the cozy retreat.

The O.S. Stapley building, a former feed store, was once the scene of an old-fashioned shootout. Another gentleman died by suicide in the building in the 1950s. These events could explain the energy that keeps the neighboring buildings highly active.

The plush One Oh One Art Gallery was once the Mesa City Bank building. The basement housed one of the original mysterious tunnels that once made a catacomb beneath Mesa city's buildings and streets. A crawl space remains to be explored, along with a staircase that leads to nowhere. Local film crews love to shoot zombie and horror movies in this location.

The owner of Mane Obsession has operated her hair salon in the same location for over twenty years. When she purchased the store, its copper ceiling tiles were all in place, but she decided a more modern look with a dropped ceiling would fit her needs better. Wanting to do a makeover, she recently thought the ceiling tiles would add a new look to her popular business. But after renovations were started, it was discovered that almost all the tiles had disappeared from under the dropped ceiling.

Some ghost hunters slipped down into the basement of the former Masonic Lodge building and found the best example of the old Mesa tunnels. Some say they were built to run bootlegged liquor during Prohibition, and some same they were used for storage and transporting merchandise under the city streets. They are now walled up, but it would be an interesting adventure to uncover what lies behind the sealed walls.

The staff at *Mystic Paper* told a story about a ghost who may have lost his marbles. Two sisters were downstairs and found a hole in the floor and asked if the ghost child kept any marbles in it. Someone dropped a nickel down the shoot to show the ladies downstairs how it all connected. The sisters came upstairs and surprised the owner by presenting them with the nickel and a marble that seemed to come from nowhere.

Next door is the home of a former butcher shop and bakery. The staff from Queen's Pizzeria and Café believe a prankster ghost rearranges items in the kitchen and sends pans flying through the air. They noted tapping on the beehive-style bricked walls. Many of the Main Street buildings still have the copper ceilings, which add to the setting. Paranormal teams have heard footsteps in the building and recorded EVPs from a ghost they call Helen.

The owners of the Evermore/Nevermore shop discovered a hidden basement when an electrician fell through while doing some rewiring. The spirits have enjoyed locking the basement and restroom doors on the owners so often that a locksmith had to be called in. The ghosts enjoy toying with the store's electronic equipment, including a CD player that must be operated

Mesa VFW Hall has a secret entrance to the tunnels. *Author's collection.*

Left: Tunnels under the VFW Hall. *Author's collection.*

Right: The stairway to the VFW Hall's basement. *Author's collection.*

manually. A mysterious man in a gray coat has been seen walking through the shop before disappearing in the back room. A search of the building could not find any lost souls in hiding.

A former Newberry's store was home to the Antique Plaza. The shop owners believed something supernatural happened in the basement. Various antique booth owners have come to work to find items tossed about the floor. Unbroken dishes have been found on the floor, still clinging to the S hooks from which they were hung on a pegboard wall. They heard knocking inside the building's walls. Employees have even heard what

The Woman's Club of Mesa, built in 1931. *Author's collection.*

sounded like heavy furniture being dragged across the floor when they were the only people in the building. Items tended to fall off the shelves and nearly hit the workers as they walked in the center aisles.

The tour ended with a stop at the eerie territorial jail cells in the back of the Arizona Museum of Natural History. The guide told the tour group that paranormal investigators have witnessed a ghostly figure coming down the stairs of the two-tiered facility. The ghost did not look happy to see a ghost hunter in the jail. Other employees have heard coughing, door slamming and unexplained noises. Witnesses say they have seen a Native

The Rydables Tour Company is the best way to see haunted Mesa. *Author's collection.*

maiden floating in the Hohokam room of the museum. Cleaning crews have heard voices and fled in the middle of the night. The statue of the Apache Gaan has been placed in several areas of the museum. Although mischief has been reported in areas he is placed, its real purpose is to teach visitors to live better lives. It was the perfect ending lesson for the historic ghost tour of Mesa.

One of the stops on the tour was Inside the Bungalow, a quaint little coffee shop on Robson Street, just north of Main Street. The ghost of a young girl has been seen sitting in the shop's back gardens. There has also been a report of a gentleman roaming from room to room inside the house, as well as on the shop's grounds. The owners suspect the spirit might be that of Mr. Openshaw, now keeping a protective eye on his former home.

These days, ghost enthusiasts can join a nightly ninety-minute tour through the haunted streets and alleys of the historic downtown Mesa district on one of the Rydables Spirited Animals. It's a captivating stuffed animal on the outside and a super-safe electric cart on the inside. Michelle Vincent and Heather Rhyneer of East Valley Paranormal lead the way past most the locations mentioned in this section. In addition, the tour includes a visit to the basement of a haunted VFW Hall and a look at the historic Mesa Women's Club House building. Specialty tours include paranormal investigations of selected locations.

QUEEN'S PIZZERIA AND CAFÉ
127 WEST MAIN STREET
MESA, AZ 85201

In recent years, Queen's Pizzeria and Café has occupied the building at 125 West Main Street in Mesa. The structure was built using Lehi brick. These adobe bricks were formed in the local Lehi area from sand and cement. Lehi bricks were not fired, making their texture very soft. Straw was sometimes mixed into the cement to help hold it together. Many of the buildings on Main Street had a coat of stucco on their exteriors and walls of brick inside to help keep their inhabitants cool.

The block of buildings, including the café, also had several former Mesa businesses within its walls. The area was once an enclosed walking breezeway. In 1911, it was listed as a butcher shop as well as a sausage

Queen's Pizzeria on Main Street. *Author's collection.*

factory. The building also housed a grocery store with an oven in the back. The grocery business decreased in size in 1923, just as the meat shop next door expanded, doubling in size.

In 1923, the address was listed as Dry Goods and Building Supplies. More spaces were added in 1924, and at one time, there were green glass tiles on its outer walls. Upton's Ice Cream Company and Upton's Malt Shop ran business there in the 1940s, and in 1952, Mollie's Fashion and Fabrics offered goods to ladies there. At least three construction phases occurred in this building. The owners were wise in their planning. They added onto only the rear of the building to avoid additional taxes.

Part of the building eventually operated as the Apache Drug Company in June 1924 and served the community until 1952. It was run by George N. Goodman, a former Mesa mayor. Goodman was president of the Arizona Pharmaceutical Association, and his wife, Clara, became the first licensed female pharmacist in Arizona.

Queen's Pizzeria opened in 2007 in the heart of downtown Mesa and was family owned. They took pride in creating fresh, delicious, made-to-order pizzas, sandwiches, wings, calzones and salads. The pizzeria made and baked its own bread and pizza dough daily. If you loved desserts, Queen's had brownies, cannoli and thrifty ice cream!

Queen's Pizzeria had been featured for several years on the annual Mesa Ghost Walk in late October. One of the tour guides told the walking groups that the building was quite active with paranormal activity. One day, after a TV crew had been there conducting an interview about the ghostly hauntings, an entire rack of pots and pans fell over the counter. Almost all the employees said they had heard knocking on the beehive-style brick walls. The former staff from Queen's Pizzeria and Café believed there was a prankster ghost that rearranged items in the kitchen and had the pans flying in the air. They also witnessed flickering lights and doors slamming, and they heard the agonizing screams of a woman searching for her children. There are undocumented tales that state there was a fire in the old shop that killed a family. What looks like burn marks from a possible fire can still be seen on the upper portions of the café's bricked walls.

The pizzeria was a big hit. It grew and expanded. The owners moved next door to a larger storefront that provided more seating for larger parties and events. The newer location of the pizzeria was filled with interesting ghost stories as well.

Until 2012, the building was the site of Evermore Nevermore Clothing and Collectibles. The previous owner confessed he began seeing unexplained phenomena the day he toured the location with the landlord. During their tour, they were surprised when the door to the women's restroom slowly opened on its own. The landlord took it in stride. He simply shrugged his shoulders as he reached over and pulled it closed again. On other occasions, the basement door locked on its own. Both restroom doors clicked and were locked by unseen hands.

Their biggest surprise came when they discovered a mysterious hidden basement. The sealed cellar was revealed when a local electrician fell through the floor while doing some rewiring at the store. Was this an old storage area, or was it used for gambling and drinking during the Prohibition era? Soon, a door was put in place that opened to a new set of stairs that led to the basement.

One day, a man dressed in a gray coat was seen walking into the busy store heading toward the back rooms. At quitting time, the owners realized they had not seen the strange man leave, so they began searching the entire store—they never found him. Later that day, a paranormal group from Tucson did an investigation and lecture in the building. A sensitive with the group said she

The tunnels under Queen's Pizzeria. *Author's collection.*

felt the presence of a man in a gray coat. That certainly caught the baffled owners off guard, especially after their visit earlier that day.

The owner also mentioned that a CD player seemed manipulated. It switched from MP3 to CD and back again on its own and turned on and off whenever it had a whim to do so. He also noticed that there was a higher chance of activity on stormy days and had seen items fly off the shelves on their own.

Debe Branning and Kenton Moore of the MVD Ghostchasers met up with two members of the Ghosts of Arizona paranormal team to investigate the newer location of the pizzeria shortly before renovations began. Lindsey Brown and his partner went down into the basement to do some EVP work while Debe and Kenton sat in the empty storefront, hoping to observe a ghostly visitor. After forty-five minutes, Debe began to visualize (in her mind's eye) a group of men entering the doors of a business from another time and walking to a back room. Perhaps the ghostly men were walking in a former alleyway between the two building additions, where people were able to engage in some nonprofessional activities. The investigation ended on a short note when Friday night revelers took over the outside walkways.

The old pizzeria building. *Author's collection.*

Michelle Vincent and Heather Rhyneer of East Valley Paranormal (and Rydables) mentioned that a group of guests on one of their tours were very intrigued by the tales of the ghost of the man in the gray coat. Several members of the tour huddled together and began to converse in almost a whisper.

"Did we say something wrong to offend you?" they asked the tour group.

"Oh, no, let me explain," one of the guests said. "Our niece was married over at the venue next door, and we decided to hold a small reception for the family over at the pizzeria. We were laughing, eating, drinking and having a good time. Suddenly, the door opened, and a man dressed in a gray coat walked in. He was nobody we invited, and none of us recognized him as a guest. We stopped and stared over at him—and suddenly, he disappeared. Now we know we were not crazy!"

Does the man in the gray coat still frequent the historic buildings as he passes through to the alleyway?

THE CHANDLER BUILDING, ALSO KNOWN AS EVERYBODY'S DRUG STORE MAIN AND MACDONALD STREETS MESA, AZ 85201

The Chandler building became the home to Everybody's Drug Store and offices when it was completed in the spring of 1908. Dr. A.J. Chandler built the first office complex in Mesa on the northwest corner of Main and MacDonald Streets using the first evaporative air-cooling system in Arizona. Another year passed before cold air equipment was utilized. To accomplish this feat, a huge fan that forced the cold draught in every room in the building was turned on. The cool air was created using the evaporation that came from water falling over coke or charcoal; a huge fan then carried the air from the cellar to the rooms. How cool was cool? The temperature was lowered in Dr. Chandler's office by something like eleven degrees, which meant the difference between the outside air and interior air of the office was roughly eleven degrees.

The new Chandler building in Mesa was the scene of a deadly fire in 1909. The building was also known as Chandler Court, referring to its courtyard architectural style. It was about 11:00 p.m. when the fire broke out in an old lumber building at the rear of the band stand near the new Chandler building.

One Mexican man was burned to death. For a while, it seemed as though the entire town of Mesa would be consumed in flames. It was only the heroic work of Mesa citizens that saved the entire town from destruction. Just what caused the fire was unknown, but it was supposed that it was started from a cigarette.

Joe Williamson was the first to see the fire and sound the alarm. He was in the rear of the barbershop when he heard someone yell, "Fire!" He looked and saw flames in an old lumber shack near the new Chandler building. He hurried closer and saw a man in the building. Thinking the man had run

Chandler Court, Mesa, Arizona.

mes matheuos
Feb. 14 1911

Mesa's Chandler courtyard, postcard. *Author's collection.*

back in to save something from the fire, Williamson rushed out on the street and sounded the alarm.

F.M. Decatur, a blacksmith at Rigg's shop, hurried to the building, and seeing that the man inside who was unable to get out, he grabbed him by the shoulders and tried to pull him out. The man's coat had been burned so much that it gave way, and Decatur was unable to get him. Decatur's hand was severely burned, and he had to seek medical treatment. Soon, the entire building was a mass of flames, and a strong wind began blowing from the west.

A large crowd of citizens gathered, and their timely work with water buckets did much to keep the fire from spreading. The fire engine also did a good job of keeping the fire under control. Several efforts were made to get the man from the building, but the heat was too intense.

Finally, the shell of the small building was pushed over, and the man's body was recovered. Dick Peterson went into the burning mass and dragged out the charred remains of the unfortunate man. His body was burned almost beyond recognition, but he was identified as Basillo Salas, also known as Chappo. He was a crippled man who was about fifty-five years old. He had been a patron of the Mesa saloons for a long time.

Those who had seen Chappo earlier that day believed he was feeling sick and probably went into the old building to lie down. The small shack was

Mesa's Chandler block. *Author's collection.*

being used by the contractors and builders of the Chandler building as a store house, and several hundred sacks of cement were piled in there along with plumbing supplies. These supplies had not been unpacked, and a great deal of excelsior was lying in the room.

It is possible that Chappo rolled a cigarette and in some way set the excelsior on fire, instantly putting the entire building in flame. Could the ghost of Chappo still be wandering about the courtyard of the Chandler building and nearby surroundings? Perhaps one will learn the answer as they stroll down Main Street late one night.

SUNSHINE LAUNDROMAT
58 SOUTH MESA DRIVE
MESA, AZ 85210

The Sunshine Laundromat is a family-owned, self-service, coin-operated laundromat located in the heart of downtown Mesa and has been serving the community for decades. It provides a clean, well-lit area with a range of machines to handle single loads and large comforters and mattress pads. There are plenty of folding tables and carts, on-site coin changers and detergent and beverage vending machines. The shop offers specials throughout the week.

Sunshine Laundromat in Mesa. *Author's collection.*

Some folks question why there would be loads of spirits inside a neighborhood laundromat. Perhaps this tale will help unfold the true mystery!

The Cahal Crew paranormal team was contacted by the manager of the Sunshine Laundromat to do an investigation concerning the unsettling activity that had recently become increasingly more agitated. Manager David and his partner, Jessica—as well as several customers—reported hearing noises in the in the back storage room. There was even a pressing issue of what sounded like the doorknob on the door at the rear of the building turning back and forth.

Upon arrival, the paranormal team set up cameras and digital recorders and cued in the Ghost Box devices to contact the spirit that may be lingering in the facility. David told the team he learned that an older gentleman who had frequented the laundromat had passed away from a heart attack in roughly 2019. The activity seemed to become a vicious cycle after that.

Debe Branning decided to tag along on the investigation, since it was not far from her home. She soon picked up on a presence near a group of dryers, specifically dryer no. 48.

"Funny you should mention that," medium Colleen Heldenbrand agreed. "On my way over here tonight, the number 48 kept popping into my head. Perhaps this is where the man died."

The group picked up on the fact that the man was a veteran and was proud he had served his country. They tried to convince the lost soldier that it would be OK to move on to the other side.

Debe's subsequent research found that a veteran had indeed suffered a heart attack at the laundromat, but he later died at a medical facility. But why does his spirit still visit the laundromat? A laundromat is a spot where the same folks meet each week to clean their clothing, have conversation and perhaps iron out some of the everyday details of their lives. It's sort of another version of *Cheers*—where everybody knows your name. Perhaps the ghostly veteran returns in the hopes that he will see his laundromat friends, or maybe he just keeps a watchful eye on the place.

The paranormal team was able to take a load of worry off the laundromat manager's mind, and ever since, everything seems to be peaceful once again.

Don't ever throw in the towel! And remember: a laundromat is merely a spin cycle of emotions and weekly wash customers.

THE MAN WHO KILLED SANTA CLAUS

Back in the late fall of 1932, a creative newspaper editor named John McPhee came up with (what he thought) was a brilliant plan to promote an upcoming pre-Christmas parade in downtown Mesa. When interest in the parade seemed rather low, he thought that a grand entrance for Santa was the way to go!

He envisioned that on December 15, 1932, a small airplane would soar through the Arizona skies and fly over the city's 2,500 residents to entertain them with a spectacular aerial acrobatics performance.

Aviation was still relatively new at the time, as was the sight of someone wearing a parachute and skydiving from a high altitude. The year before, the City of Phoenix had arranged for Santa to arrive via an airplane. But that Santa simply disembarked from a grounded aircraft. To see Santa jump out of a plane would be quite the sensation for the Mesa community!

The December 9, 1932 *Journal-Tribune* newspaper read:

> *The generous old gentleman isn't coming in the conventional style, and he isn't going to wait until the airplane lands to get out. He is going to drop right down in the center of Mesa on a parachute. He'll be here at 4:15 o'clock next Friday afternoon, December 16, with a greeting and a present for every Mesa kiddie who is downtown to see him. Every kid in the Mesa district is invited to be in Mesa next Friday afternoon and help show Santa a good time. Santa's airplane will arrive over Mesa direct from the North Pole at exactly 4:15 o'clock. His pilot will circle the airplane over Mesa rooftops and will put the plane through a few difficult stunts. Then Santa will step out on the wing and with his special parachute firmly attached to his body, he will step off to land in the arms of the awaiting children.*

It was carefully planned so that at precisely 4:15 p.m., the small plane's cargo door would slowly open to reveal Santa Claus! Well, he would appear more like a professional stuntman dressed in the familiar red Santa suit and his famous white beard. Santa would leap from the plane at about three thousand feet using a parachute to make his descent to a nearby alfalfa field on the outskirts of town. A police escort would be waiting for the skydiver, and he would be whisked back to the business district of Mesa so he could hand out a bag full of holiday presents, nuts and candy!

Well, at least that was the plan. The town newspaper the *Mesa Journal-Tribune* printed updates on the story, and it was all anyone—especially the schoolchildren—could talk about. This was the middle of the Great Depression, so all the storekeepers on Main Street anticipated a big sales day! Children were delighted at such a dangerous stunt taken on by Santa. Mr. McPhee was the hero of the day!

But less than a week later, McPhee was being run out of town. For the remaining thirty-six years of his life, he would be known as the man who killed Santa Claus.

Apparently, Mr. McPhee's stuntman Santa had a totally different idea of his own. On the day of the big event, McPhee found the performer seated at a local bar much too inebriated to leap from an airplane—parachute or not! Fearing he would be run out of town by storekeepers, parents and disappointed children, McPhee had to come up with another plan. He borrowed a mannequin from a clothing store and dressed it in the coveted Santa suit. He loaded the dummy Santa into the plane and instructed the pilot to do the scheduled flight. When it was time for Santa to jump, the pilot was to simply push the red-suited Santa out of the plane and into the awaiting alfalfa field.

McPhee assumed that, from a distance, the spectators would not be able to determine the plastic mannequin body from a real one. They would see the form of the red and white body drift slowly to the ground. McPhee planned to be at the site to meet the dummy, change into the suit and beard and drive into Mesa as Santa!

But that's not exactly what happened.

Later that afternoon, the residents of Mesa began to gather along the sidewalks downtown. Their necks were craned to look for any sign of the airplane carrying the precious cargo, Santa Claus. Children climbed nearby telephone poles and their fathers' shoulders. Mothers pointed up to sky as they tried to keep the small tots busy. Store owners readied their businesses for a huge evening of sales.

The plane started doing circles around the town and over the rooftops. As advertised, a red-suited Santa appeared in the cockpit doorway. There were cheers! Nobody seemed to notice that the man was less than animated. It was Santa at last!

The old-timers of Mesa would later recall the turnout for Santa's arrival was "the largest crowd in its history"—but this would be a rather unfortunate fact. Santa stepped off the plane right on cue, but the mannequin began rocketing through the air! McPhee, who was watching from the nearby pasture, expected to see a parachute like those in a typical military cargo drop. But nothing was slowing this Santa's descent. He fell like a dead weight! The parachute did not open.

As Santa rocketed to what was seemingly his untimely death, the children began to scream! Some parents covered their babies' eyes, their own mouths wide open in disbelief of what was occurring in front of them. Santa was led off course. He crash-landed in a lettuce field.

McPhee, still in shock, raced toward the dummy, stripped it of the red suit and dressed as Santa so he could begin consoling eyewitnesses. A few minutes later, Santa was seen riding through town on the hood of the city police car driven by Marshall Ray Merrill. He arrived to a veritable ghost town—children were behind doors, sobbing. McPhee thought they would be calmed by the sight of Santa alive and well, but no one knew how to react. The parade went on as scheduled, but it more resembled a funeral procession.

What really went wrong? Maybe we will never really know. It was not revealed by the *Journal-Tribune* until several years later, when the newspaper's former editor John McPhee died.

John McPhee's obituary explained:

> *It was while working on a Mesa Chamber of Commerce project that he became known as "the man who killed Santa Claus." The chamber had hired a man to parachute in a Santa suit, but on the appointed day, he was drunk and unable to perform his duties.*
>
> *McPhee hit upon the idea of releasing a store manikin in a Santa suit from an airplane, with another man to take over on the ground and greet the children. When the manikin was pushed out of the plane, the parachute failed to open, and horrified children and adults watched the supposed Santa plunge to the ground.*

Parents were so concerned their children had been traumatized by seeing Santa meet his maker that the boys and girls of Mesa were showered with presents that year. Perhaps this is now just a ghost of Christmas past.

ARIZONA MUSEUM OF NATURAL HISTORY
53 NORTH MACDONALD STREET
MESA, AZ 85201

The Arizona Museum of Natural History was originally founded as a small museum at the former Mesa City Hall in 1977, containing a small collection of Arizona artifacts. The building was designed by Lescher and Mahoney. It was built in 1937 with WPA funds and originally housed Mesa City Hall, municipal courts, the city library and both the fire and police departments—along with the city jail. There were expansions to the building in 1983 and 1987, and in 2000, a new wing was added. The main museum complex currently comprises about seventy-four thousand square feet, of which about forty-six thousand square feet are dedicated to exhibitions containing a collection of about sixty thousand objects of natural history, anthropology, history and art, with approximately ten thousand historic photographs. A research facility was also added in 1995. Additionally, the museum has prominent research curators in the fields of paleontology and archeology/anthropology.

The museum has a popular three-story indoor waterfall on Dinosaur Mountain, which features animatronic dinosaurs and offers a flash flood presentation that runs every thirty minutes. Guests can enjoy Dinosaur Hall and a re-creation of the Lost Dutchman's Gold Mine. One can also pan for gold on the outdoor patio in the courtyard. The Southwest Gallery has a Native peoples' gallery with changing exhibits. There is a re-creation of a Hohokam village with pit houses and aboveground structures, complete with artifacts from about 600–1450 CE. Another exhibit is called the *Ancient Cultures of Mexico*. The Origins Gallery offers a voyage through the timeline of the cosmos and discusses major events in the history of Earth.

But one of the most talked-about displays, tucked in the far back corner of the building, is the old territorial city jail. Some visitors to the museum believe the cells, with their old iron bars, are haunted.

Back in the 1880s Maricopa County purchased an assembled-on-site, two-story jail to house local criminals in Phoenix. The Maricopa County Jail was built in 1883 and constructed as the main cell block of the old

Arizona Museum of Natural History. *Author's collection.*

Mesa City Jail. *Courtesy of Flickr.*

territorial courthouse in Phoenix. The jail housed cattle rustlers, horse thieves and desperados who were jailed during Arizona's wild territorial days. The sheriff from 1909 to 1912 was Carol Hayden, who later became an Arizona senator.

In 1936, the county deputy sheriff in Mesa became aware that the Maricopa County Board of Supervisors was planning to give three sets of cells to other county branch facilities. He arranged for Mesa to acquire the main block, and for the $265 cost of transporting twelve of those original cells from Phoenix, the City of Mesa had a new jail. It served as a county and city jail until its closure in 1975, when the new Mesa Police building was completed. The cells on exhibit have been carefully preserved intact—except the bars were once made of cold black steel and the walls were bare cement.

Prisoners received two cold meals a day that usually consisted of a cup of coffee and a sandwich. They slept on bare steel bunks with no bedding. No mattresses or blankets were provided because prisoners would often set fire to them and endanger other inmates. There were nineteen bunks on the lower level, yet there were times when as many as seventy men were packed into the cell block to await arraignment. The excessive overcrowding occurred on the weekends when court was not held. Women were housed in a small separate room with two windows. They were provided with bedding and had a shower as well as a commode in their facility.

The jail cells have held on to some of the residual energies of the prisoners who did their time here. Volunteers at the historic jail exhibit say it is the scariest spot in the huge seventy-four-thousand-square-foot

Opposite: Old Mesa City Jail. *Author's collection.*

Above: The Old Mesa City Jail's cells. *Author's collection.*

Right: The jail cells are now part of a museum. *Author's collection.*

museum. Many of these volunteers will not go into the exhibit without a partner. They often hear footsteps echoing along the iron floor, and others have seen ghostly apparitions and shadows moving about the jail cells.

There were several prisoners who attempted to escape from the old jail. What would cause them to risk their own lives? Was there something haunting them from the cellblock's early history?

At 11:30 p.m. on February 22, 1918, a Mesa officer named Pickens placed a prisoner, George McDaniels, in the inner cell until morning. But when Pickens arrived at the jail the next morning, he found the bars sawed in two and McDaniels gone. Pickens made for the McDanielses' home and discovered George hiding in the shade of a pepper tree. After escaping from jail, McDaniels had hurried home and changed his suit to wait for an auto to arrive to whisk him away. The officer took him back to jail, where he again sat confined in the inner cell.

There were several more escape attempts over the years; one prisoner even tried to dig his way out with a spoon. On January 4, 1921, three inmates tried to escape through the ceiling, cutting it in three different places. But in each case, the prisoners met with iron bars that blocked their freedom and were forced to stop. You see, early on, two other men cut a hole through the ceiling and into the floor of the courtroom in city hall, which forced additional bars to be installed. Perhaps the ghostly spirits in the jail are the former inmates still doing time in the escape-proof cellblock!

GHOST HUNT AT THE ANTIQUE PLAZA
114 AND 120 WEST MAIN STREET
MESA, AZ 85201

A group of ghost investigators attended a MVD Ghostchasers Spirit Workshop on August 13, 2011, and were treated to a late-night investigation of the Antique Plaza in Mesa, Arizona. At the request of the plaza's former owner, a smaller than usual investigation team covered the two-story antique wonderland from top to bottom. Armed with various types of cameras, recording devices and several types of EMF meters, a night of ghost hunting and debunking was soon underway.

Formerly a busy J.J. Newberry's department store that opened in May 1949 on Main Street, the building eventually became the home of Antique

Plaza in 1993. The old 1949 lunch counter, minus the swiveling barstools, was a mainstay for many years. The building comprised twenty-two thousand square feet, which included a basement, unusual for Arizona. It boasted high ceilings to promote air conditioning, and many former employees remember the creepy old freight elevator in the back that led up to a partial second floor.

The shop owners believed most of the supernatural activity occurred in the basement. Various antique booth owners came to work to find items tossed about the floor. Unbroken dishes were found off the walls, still clinging to the S hooks that were secured to a pegboard. They heard knocking inside the building's walls. Employees sometimes heard heavy furniture being dragged across the tile floor when they were alone in the store. Items tended to fall off the shelves, nearly hitting the workers as they strolled along the center aisles. Several folks noticed a shadowy presence walking in the basement. Other sellers reported unexplained sounds, smells and sightings of figures and items being moved around the building's spacious rooms. Some believe the spirit could be that of a former Newberry's employee who worked in the store until it closed and just never wanted to give up the job they loved.

The first exercise of the investigative evening was a take on the TV show *Haunted Collector*. Sometimes it has been learned that an antique can be possessed by something that happened in the past or perhaps its previous owner. The teams broke up into pairs and combed each aisle to search for those irregular trigger objects that emitted high EMF readings or might be holding the haunting energies of their past owners. This was also the perfect way to do a sweep of the building to seek out power surges, other electronic devices or panel boxes discharging energy.

And the crew was able to debunk nearly every power surge that registered on the EMF meters. They were mostly caused by overhead florescent lights, cooling fans in adjoining booths or distorted ballast lights in some of the display cases.

Next, the group gathered near the bottom of the stairs that lead down to the basement area for an EVP session. Earlier, three members of the group had heard what sounded like a large dog panting near them close to the basement area. Although each of the investigators heard the panting at various times, they all agreed it felt like the presence of a medium-sized dog. A second EVP session was held in the basement after lights-out.

Later, with only the light of the full moon to guide them, the investigators made another sweep of the two-story building filming with infrared cameras and snapping digital shots of various antique booths and displays.

Is the Antique Plaza haunted? Although the eighty-year-old building might not be haunted itself, it is almost certain some of the items on display may be carrying some mojo from its previous iterations. The owner of the store reported that, once, the basement held a negative energy that focused on a particular chair. Nobody wanted to go down in the basement for any reason. After the chair was finally sold, a lighter, more refreshing atmosphere again filled the spacious store.

We should remember that all the photographs, fine crystal, chinaware, clothing and collectibles were once someone's pride and joy. Perhaps Grandma came along with these fine items from her estate sale and is having a hard time letting her items go to new homes. Her energy could be causing the movement of the items or the sudden noises in the store. There are also spirits that love lots of attention, and they could be emitting an energy to say, "Hey, you! Come here and look—you should buy this!"

Whatever the case may be, take a walk around the store yourself. You just might find a mysterious item you were not expecting to purchase that just grabs you. And you can always call the haunted collector if it holds on too tight!

THE NILE THEATER
105 WEST MAIN STREET
MESA, AZ 85210

The Nile Theater opened on September 2, 1924, along Main Street as Mesa's grandest and only movie palace. The *Arizona Republican* explained the theater's origin in this way: "Following a thought that has often appeared that the Salt River valley of Arizona is the only rival to the fertile Nile region, the management of the theater conceived the idea of naming their house after the historic river of Egypt and carrying out in every way a comprehensive Egyptian plan even in the minutest detail of decoration for its opening."

Constructed at a time when the world was fascinated by ancient Egypt, the Nile Theater initially displayed an artistic design that was reflective of the popular Art Deco and Egyptian motifs seen in other buildings from this era. It had a sloping floor, center stage and the best cooling system. The theater was notably the first known air-cooled building in Arizona and served as inspiration for other entertainment venues in the valley. It boasted

Nile Theater, opened in 1924. *Author's collection.*

a large box far back under the theater's stage that was filled with huge blocks of ice. A fan behind it helped blow cool air through ventilation tunnels that led to small grills along the floor.

"The construction of the Nile Theater inspired the construction of other theaters within the valley, including the Orpheum Theater that was built four years later in Phoenix," city records state.

The lavish Egyptian-themed Nile Theater opened in 1924, five years before Phoenix's Orpheum Theater, when Mesa's population was less than four thousand. The Nile was a collaborative effort of the three leading movie moguls of the valley: Jo E. Rickards, Harry L. Nace and William Menhennet.

The Nile closed as a movie theater in 1951 as the Tri-Cities area began to expand and develop. It lived on with other uses, including as a clothing store and later as a nightclub at the center of the valley's punk scene in the early 2000s. It was the home of Faith Harvest Church until it was sold in 2010 and reopened as a rock concert venue.

Nile Theater owner Michelle Donovan invited the paranormal team East Valley Paranormal to investigate some ongoing activity that had been reported by employees and visiting bands. Heather Rhyneer and Michele Vincent immediately set up their paranormal equipment and recorded some of the best data they had ever gotten.

"It was one EVP right after another," Heather reported. "Men, women, children, old folks, young folks—it was almost as if they were all talking at once! I think the spirits were happy someone had come to visit."

After an evening of investigating, the duo was amazed at what they found on their digital video camera the next day. Up high in the rafters, a woman in white was seen leaning over to look at them. She was known as the "lady in the rafters" by others who had thought they witnessed her in the past, and the EVP team could not believe their eyes. They played their footage repeatedly and even came back to the theater to reshoot their photographs to make sure they had not encountered a lighting issue or something that looked like a woman. Nothing appeared on their cameras from the second filming.

Some of the EVPs the paranormal team recorded said, "I want that dress back," "I said you could wear the hat" and "I've been hit." Whether they were voices from previous businesses, theater patrons or folks enjoying a night listening to music, we may never know. But there is no doubt the Nile is no longer a silent movie palace.

Aside from changes to the theater's marquee and box office structure, the property still looks quite the same as it did when it opened nearly a century ago. The Nile still operates as a popular music venue and coffee shop.

BUCKHORN HOT MINERAL BATHS MOTEL
5900 EAST MAIN STREET
MESA, AZ 85205

The Buckhorn Hot Mineral Baths Motel is located at the corner of Main Street and Recker Road in East Mesa. It began as a small gas station and store in 1936. Ted and Alice Sliger upgraded the property to become an oasis resort complex that opened in 1939 and was finally complete by 1947.

It was a small mineral hot springs resort that offered a bathhouse as well as cottages and motel rooms for overnight travelers. The buildings were all designed in the Pueblo Revival style. The motel continued to operate after the bathhouse closed until 1999. The motel and its wildlife museum continued as a business until 2004. The Buckhorn Motel was added to the National Register of Historic Places in 2005.

Ted Sliger's early store and lunch counter in Mesa, Desert Wells, burned to the ground in 1936, destroying his large collection of taxidermy except for one buckhorn deer, which was on loan at the time. Ted and Alice purchased a ten-acre piece of property in the open desert, just seven miles east of Mesa. They eventually added more parcels of land to the west and north of the motel. They bought a house from a neighbor and had it moved to the property. The couple constructed the store from bricks they scavenged from an old, demolished Mesa school. From the store, they sold gasoline, groceries, hunting and fishing licenses, fishing tackle and beautiful Native jewelry and rugs.

In 1938, they expanded the store to display Ted's taxidermy work once again. It was a service he loved providing to local hunters and fisherman. It soon evolved into a new wildlife museum, showcasing over four hundred specimens of wildlife.

The couple had to haul in all their drinking water and eventually decided it would be easier to dig a well. In 1939, the Sligers sunk their well and were surprised to find the water they struck was 112 degree Fahrenheit mineral water. To prosper from their new find, they built a bathhouse with the capacity to serve seventy-five people. They added new cottages to accommodate guests who wished to stay overnight. They named their new business Buckhorn after that one piece of Ted's taxidermy that had been saved from the earlier fire.

The roadway that ran past the Sligers' property became Highway 60, now Mesa's East Main Street. It became an important tourist road in the Salt River valley, connecting the Tri-Cities together. It connected Phoenix to various recreational and tourist areas and to the small mining towns east of Mesa. The Buckhorn was well-placed in an area that attracted automobile tourism after the end of the Depression. Automobile tourist facilities were becoming increasingly visible in most cities across the United States. These rest havens would soon become the more sophisticated motel, a motor court with some of the amenities of a hotel.

Between 1940 and 1947, the Sligers improved and extended their motel business by expanding the bathhouse. They eventually closed the gas station

Buckhorn Baths Hot Springs. *Author's collection.*

and removed the porte-cochere, which had sheltered the gas pumps. They added a large sandstone-supported neon sign that advertised the "Buckhorn Hot Mineral Baths Motel," which gave it the look one sees today.

Sometime during World War II, additional double cottages were moved to the property, west of the original site, which increased the size of the resort. The motel additionally became a Greyhound bus depot in 1942. In 1947, the New York Giants baseball team (and, later, the Chicago Cubs) selected the Buckhorn as their base of operations during the annual spring training season. The bus depot closed in 1972, the same year that the Giants moved on to a hotel in Casa Grande.

When viewed from Main Street, the front structure appears to be one building. It is surprisingly a collection of several individual buildings. The office/owner's residence and the museum/lobby share a common wall, but the roof of each is separate. The post office and store office were located in separate buildings with walkways between that provide access from the front parking lot to the interior of the complex. All the units share an arcade and parapet, and most importantly, their Pueblo Revival mortared stones and metates (Native grindstones) were used to build walls and other decorative objects on the grounds.

In its glory days, the Buckhorn Motel could easily house one hundred vacationing guests. It offered a café and dining room, a gift shop, a beauty salon and, of course, the taxidermy museum, which also displayed Native relics. It also offered a lobby and television room and an indoor cactus garden. The motel offered amenities such as an eighteen-hole desert golf course, a fireplace/barbecue area and a shuffleboard court. The desert oasis grounds featured manicured lawns, palm trees and other foliage and decorative pools and fountains. Four additional mineral springs wells were dug, and by 1974, the bathhouse had separate entrances for men and women and twenty-seven private baths, as well as whirlpool baths and massage and cooling rooms. The resort employed trained masseurs and masseuses, physical therapists and nurses, all dressed in white uniforms. The mineral water in the baths was 106 degrees Fahrenheit.

After the death of Ted Sliger in 1984, Alice Sliger continued to run the resort. Buckhorn Baths closed in 1999, and the motel and museum closed in 2004. Some of the motel units continued to be occupied as apartments, and security live on the site as of today.

Urban legend speculates that Elvis Presley spent the night at the famous Buckhorn Baths Motel during the time the "King of Rock 'n' Roll" was filming scenes for the 1960 movie *Flaming Star*. Some folks believe his ghost frequents the grounds. Like George Washington, Elvis has a reputation for sleeping at many historic locations, and Mesa Buckhorn Mineral Baths can be added to the long list. Elvis did come to Mesa to visit his old friend Tom Diskin, who co-owned Jamboree Productions in Memphis, Tennessee, and was one of Colonel Parker's right-hand men. After all, the mineral bathhouse would have been the perfect retreat after a long day of shooting scenes for a movie. There are no records of Elvis checking into the motel, but he did lead a mysterious secret life. One may never know!

Rob Koller of PAPS (Phoenix Arizona Paranormal Society) investigated the Buckhorn for ghostly activity in 2012. The team was blown away by all the spirit activity at the site. Rob noted there were at least five documented deaths at the hotel. Former owner Alice Sliger told a few interested parties that she believed someone had probably died in almost every cabin over the years.

In recent years, a couple who were caretakers at the Buckhorn had their own encounter with the ghosts. They lived on the property in unit 17, which gave them the perfect view of folks who were trespassing or had wandered onto the grounds. The wife of the on-site caretaker reported getting out of bed one night and meeting face to face with a tall, dapper man in cowboy gear strolling through their room. No contact was made. No words were exchanged, and no harm was intended. The peaceful spirit simply walked about the room as if it was his, tipped his cowboy hat and slowly faded away.

PAPS paranormal investigator Jamie Veik noted,

> *Our team has investigated the Buckhorn Baths several times and even conducted a few tours there several years back. This place is one of our*

all-time favorite locations, based on the history alone. Ted and Alice Sliger opened this business nearly one hundred years ago, and a lot of their possessions remained in the building. There is so much evidence, it is remarkable. I would say that this location is probably the most haunted location in the East Valley, if not all of Phoenix. We have on video the K-2 meter moving on its own while pegging to "red." A calendar that has been hanging on the wall for thirty years seemingly unscrewed itself and fell on the head of one of our tour guests. These two incidents happened in the female massage parlor, where it's been told a masseuse died back in the 1960s. We have captured shadow figures, bizarre light anomalies (not orbs), and in the restaurant building on a random Saturday morning, while quietly walking around when no one was talking, one of our investigators captured what sounded like a little girl running on a hard wood floor. She completely stopped and said, "I have to go to the bathroom." And right after that, a woman's voice said, "There is no bathroom." It was a class A EVP, although a residual EVP—it was still incredible.

The famous Buckhorn Hot Mineral Baths Motel has long been closed. Although the taxidermy animals and artifacts have long been removed from Buckhorn Baths, there is still hope that someone will step up and bring this historic landmark back to life. And although Elvis has definitely left the building, the watchful eyes of the current caretakers have not. Please, no trespassing!

3

TEMPE

TEMPE FOR THE WORLD

Tempe has been a small agricultural community for most of its history, growing crops and raising livestock. After World War II, Tempe grew at a rapid rate as soldiers and veterans returned and began moving to the city to rear their families. Eventually, the farms disappeared. The city of Tempe reached its landlocked boundaries by 1974.

Between 500 and 1450 CE, prehistoric Hohokam people created a large desert canal system off the Salt River. Hints of their culture remain today in the ruins of their dwellings, pottery shards, artifacts and petrographs carved in the surrounding rock formations.

Father Eusebio Kino, a Jesuit missionary, named the river Rio Salado, Spanish for "salt," because of the salty taste its waters have. Even as late as the 1800s, the Salt River flowed uncontrolled, blocking the trailways that led from Phoenix to Tucson. Many of the farmers, ranchers and immigrants who settled near the river carefully made use of their important water source.

Charles Trumbull Hayden started the vital Hayden Ferry crossing at the Salt River narrows, which is near what is now downtown Tempe. Hayden's flour mill made use of the water flowing through the canals from the river. He built his house and trading post as a port for the ferry service. His home was offered as lodging, and he provided food for weary travelers.

Tempe was officially named after the Greek Vale of Tempe from mythology in 1879. By 1885, the territorial legislature had decided the Territorial Normal School would be built in Tempe. It is now the highly academic Arizona State University (ASU). Tempe, the dynamic home to ASU, boasts the motto "Tempe for the World!"

Above: Tempe is located along the thirty-third parallel (33.2341). *Author's collection.*

Left: Historic Mill Avenue. *Courtesy of Pinterest.*

GHOSTLY DUEL BETWEEN TEMPE AND MESA

The Tempe Canal Path parallels the Tempe Canal between the cities of Tempe and Mesa.

The Tempe Canal is the oldest continuously used canal in the Salt River's canal system. Construction of the Tempe Canal was undertaken by the Tempe Irrigating Canal Company, which had originally been incorporated in 1870 as the Hardy Irrigating canal Company. Its name was changed the following year.

A shoot-out took place on the roadway, halfway between Tempe and Mesa, Arizona, one summer afternoon in 1906. A rancher named Williams lay dead with his head frightfully torn apart by a gunshot wound fired by another rancher named Weller, the husband of William's former wife. After Williams and the woman divorced, she married Weller, and as one can imagine, the feuding began to grow.

This tragic event took place around high noon and was witnessed by several persons who were traveling the road between the two East Valley cities, near the banks of the Tempe Canal.

It was reported that there had been bad blood between Williams and Weller for quite some time. Both men had bad temperaments and felt jealousy over their coveted spouse. They are said to have confronted each other with gunplay before.

On that morning, their paths crossed at the halfway point near the Tempe Canal. Williams declared that he would "fill Weller so full of bullet holes that a dog could jump through him." Williams tried to make a bluff by reaching for his gun near his hip pocket. But Weller was not bluffing. He pulled out a shotgun and fired directly at Williams. He used both barrels, and the bullets struck Williams in the head, killing him almost instantly.

Ever wonder why you suddenly get a chill as you cross over the Tempe Canal? They say the canals in Arizona hold a powerful intensity for hauntings. Gunfights such as this could be one of the reasons why.

A.J. MATTHEWS CENTER
ARIZONA STATE UNIVERSITY
950 CADY MALL
TEMPE, AZ 85281

Originally the first library on campus, the A.J. Matthews Center continues to represent the spirit of learning and creativity at ASU. The School of Human Evolution and Social Change maintains archaeological and physical anthropology collections, meeting spaces and student and faculty offices in the building. Student Media, where students publish the *State Press*, the campus daily and the seventh-largest publication in Arizona, is located in Matthews Center. Comprehensive support services for students with disabilities, including alternative print formats and interpreting, are provided by Disability Resources.

The building was constructed in 1930 and named for ASU president Arthur John Matthews, the first in ASU history to serve with the title president. Matthews held this title from 1900 to 1930.

In October 2002, the MVD Ghostchasers were invited by staff to investigate the hauntings of the Matthews Center. Their mission was to search for spirits and investigate the stories that have puzzled ASU for many years, including the

ASU's A.J. Matthews Center, built in 1930. *Author's collection.*

narrow back staircases and tunnels that can be accessed from the basement. Some of the paranormal team members felt uneasy on the fifth-floor landing of the back staircase. They said they smelled the faint odor of smoke and a burning sensation in their throats. A light turned itself back on after being set in the off position. They felt as if someone was watching them when they stood on the rooftop to catch the full moon and view of the campus.

The investigators were told the Matthews Center was once the university's main library and that the *Hayden's Ferry Review* office downstairs was used as an autopsy room when the building became home to nursing students.

The staff told the MVD Ghostchasers the undocumented legend of a librarian who perished in a fire when she was trapped on the back stairways of the Matthews Center building. Some workers and students in the center have seen a woman wandering the stairs searching for an exit.

The group was also told that the anthropology department kept Native bones in the building. The U.S. military was said to have given ASU Native bones to study, after which people started seeing the ghosts of Apache warriors wandering the halls late at night. Once the bones were returned to their appropriate tribes, the activity began to cease. An anthropology professor stepped up to note that the only bones worth mentioning belonged to the bodies of two gorillas—not Natives, as rumored.

A gorilla, Jack, was flown into the Phoenix Zoo via Hugh Heffner's private plane to serve as companion for Phoenix's famous gorilla Hazel. Jack died of valley fever soon after his arrival, and his bones were donated to ASU's anthropology department. The professor said he had never seen the ghost of the gorilla but may have heard Jack's haunting primate holler late at night.

Many students and staff have heard variations of the tale of the ghostly librarian. Some say she burned in a fire in the building. Others say she died off campus in a horrific car accident. And still others claim she died by suicide. No matter her cause of death, many have seen a female figure wandering through the hallways. No record has been found to document her death, but almost everyone has heard the story or knows someone who claims to have seen the ghostly apparition. One employee who worked in the basement of Matthews Center starting in 1979 claimed she heard the librarian burned along with a fireman who tried to rescue her on a back staircase.

The MVD Ghostchasers told the staff, "She didn't have to die here in order to make her presence here. Perhaps she comes back to the center because she loved her job and it was a location she really liked."

The crew who worked in the basement area reported hearing sounds coming from the other side of a door that led out to the massive

ASU's A.J. Matthews Center. *Author's collection.*

underground tunnels underneath the buildings on campus. A small group of paranormal investigators entered the dark area with flashlights and wandered through the never-ending tunnel system. They debunked the noises saying they came from the water and electrical and cable lines. The team returned and assured the workers they had nothing to fear. But they had a great time exploring those catacombs!

Comedian Jerry Lewis visited the ASU campus and enjoyed a few scenes outside the Matthews Library while filming *The Nutty Professor* in 1962. In the movie, he asks, "What happen to you last night? What'd you run away like that for? I thought you saw a ghost or something!"

VIRGINIA G. PIPER CENTER FOR CREATIVE WRITING
ARIZONA STATE UNIVERSITY
450 EAST TYLER MALL
TEMPE, AZ 85281

The Virginia G. Piper Writers' House was built in 1907 and served as the home of several ASU presidents. Arthur John Matthews (1904–30), Ralph W. Swetman (1930–33) and Grady Gammage (1933–59) resided in the

Left: ASU's Old Main is the scene of many photo shoots. *Author's collection.*

Below: ASU's Old Main, built in 1898. *Author's collection.*

historic president's cottage until it became the Alumni House and Alumni Executive Office (1961–72). Most recently, the building has been the home of the University Archives (1972–95).

In 2005, the building saw more renovations, including the addition of lavish gardens and a back patio. It now serves as the Virginia G. Piper Center for Creative Writing, which offers offices for staff, creative writing classrooms and a gathering space for readings, receptions and events.

Along with the impressive University Club and Old Main, the Piper Writers' House is one of the few remaining historic buildings on the ASU–Tempe campus. The house was one of the last buildings designed by the popular territorial architect James Creighton, who also designed the original ASU Normal School (now demolished).

The president's house is a symmetrical, two-story, Western Colonial brick building with a copper shingle roof. The central entry was originally a projecting hipped porch with classical detailing. The porch was enclosed in 1937 with four-lite casement windows and a twelve-lite entry door with eight-pane side lights. The main house has a two-story bay window on its west side and a two-story bay with fireplace on its east side. The roof boasts projecting gables and featured boxed eaves and a central hipped dormer. In 1931, two rooms and a bath were added to the northwest corner.

One of its spirited residents is the ghost of Dixie Gammage, the wife of ASU president Dr. Grady Gammage, who passed away in an upstairs bedroom in December 1959.

The popular couple met in Prescott, Arkansas, fell in love and were married. They relocated to Tucson, Arizona, where Grady attended the university. After Grady's graduation, he and Dixie went to Winslow, where he became the superintendent of Winslow schools. From Winslow, the couple moved to Flagstaff in 1925, following Dr. Gammage's appointment to the presidency of the Arizona State College there. The Gammage family were living in Tempe when Dr. Gammage became the president of the college campus.

Known for her civic and social activities, Dixie Gammage was a past president of the Tempe Woman's Club and a member of the Tempe Methodist Church. She was very active in community affairs until ill health forced her to give up many of her duties.

Dixie became an invalid and was confined to the second floor of the house, where she spent a good many of her last days. She traveled to Paradise Valley Sanatorium near San Diego, California, for health reasons in August 1948. She was sixty-four years old and had been under

The Virginia G. Piper Center for Creative Writing at ASU. *Author's collection.*

treatment for heart and liver ailments. She passed away at the sanatorium on September 11 that year. Soon after her death, she was purportedly seen on occasion walking past the second-story windows of her former Tempe home dressed in a bathrobe and wearing a hat.

A gentleman who was the former university archivist at the ASU library often reported ghostly happenings at both the Matthews Center and the Virginia G. Piper Center. He claimed he had a paranormal experience in the Piper Writers' House when it was used as the archives building between the 1980s and 1990s. His office was located across the hall from the southwestern corner bedroom where President Grady Gammage died. He remembered hearing a creaky door close downstairs while he was working upstairs late at night. He went down the stairs looking for a possible explanation but did not find the cause—or an intruder!

Grady Gammage was born in Arkansas in August 1892. He died of a heart attack on the morning of December 22, 1959, as his physician was examining him. Gammage had complained he was very tired and was not feeling well the night before. His death came unexpectedly; he was sixty-seven years old. Grady Gammage was honored with lying in state beneath the rotunda at the Arizona State Capitol. He was buried at Greenwood Cemetery in Phoenix.

Another university spokesperson noted that he heard stories that ghostly apparitions have been seen in the building, along with lights turning on late at night. A group of students known as the Devils Advocates, in the 1990s, gave tours to prospective students, new enrollees and their parents throughout the year. The volunteer guides told stories of the past, sometimes adding a little folklore to the tales. They, too, believed the president's home is haunted and jokingly relayed a rumor that Mrs. Gammage used to sunbathe in the nude on the roof!

AN ENCHANTED GHOST EUCHRE PARTY
ARIZONA STATE UNIVERSITY
UNIVERSITY DRIVE AND MILL AVENUE
TEMPE, AZ 85281

Looking for something new to do at a Halloween get-together this fall? Back in 1891, the latest craze in Tempe, Arizona, was a progressive ghost Euchre party. Euchre is a trick-taking card game and is commonly played with four people in two partnerships with a deck of twenty-four standard playing cards. You can almost imagine the excitement of this game being played on the haunted Temple Normal School campus!

Guests arrived at the party, and not a word was spoken until the twelve games of Euchre were played and the prizes were won. Sheets and full-curtain masks were worn, and none of the players knew who their card-playing partners were. Try to picture what an awfully weird and altogether unsocial affair this friendly game of cards must have been under these ghostly circumstances!

The following are instructions for how to play a spirit channeling game called Ghost. Ghost is a game in which you can channel a spirit or spirits and ask questions. You will not see or hear the spirits, but they will talk to you through your deck of playing cards.

Create a circle of protection to keep you safe from any unwanted energies. Some say to light a white or blue protective candle. Spirits are drawn to fire, so perhaps the more candles you have, the easier and more fun the game will be.

Shuffle the cards and lay as many as you want on the floor or the surface you are playing on. Choose one person to be the medium. The medium will ask the question for the spirits to answer. As the questions are asked, the medium will wave their hands over the cards to pick up the energy submitted by the spirits. Flip over the card the energy indicates and get your answer.

This is the code: hearts, yes; spades, no; diamonds, maybe; clubs, I don't know.

If you notice that the questions or answers are too vague, switch mediums. The game is a fun experience and can create an entertaining story to share with others.

DOUBLE BUTTE CEMETERY GHOSTLY PIONEERS
2505 WEST BROADWAY ROAD
TEMPE, AZ 85282

The Double Butte Cemetery is the official name given to a historic cemetery in Tempe, Arizona. The cemetery was founded in 1888 near the base of the Double Butte Mountain, for which it is named. It is the final resting place of several notable pioneers of the city of Tempe. The cemetery, which is located south of Broadway Road, is listed in the Tempe Historic Property Register, designation no. 46. The location of the cemetery was chosen because it was situated several miles from the Tempe town limits and because the towering butte served as a prominent geographical marker. The pioneer section of the cemetery was listed in the National Register of Historic Places on July 30, 2013.

Double Butte Cemetery was established on September 13, 1897. Many Tempe residents and those who played key roles in the history of the state

Double Butte Cemetery. *Courtesy of Find a Grave.*

of Arizona are interred at Double Butte Cemetery. Sections A, B, C and D are the areas of the graveyard in which the Tempe Cemetery Company first began selling family lots. It is now known as the Pioneer Section.

Many of the burials where the present cemetery is located occurred far before the official establishment of the cemetery. Local citizens formed a group called the Tempe Cemetery Association to maintain growing burial records. The property was donated by Niels Petersen in 1888 (see the section on the Petersen House). Petersen himself was buried at Double Butte Cemetery until 1923. It is then that his remains were exhumed and reinterred on the property where his historic house is located.

For the next decade, Double Butte Cemetery grew to become Tempe's primary burial place. The economic situation in the 1920s and 1930s caused troubled times for the cemetery. The Tempe Cemetery Company was in dire financial straits, and sadly, the cemetery suffered immensely as a result. Grave sites were found sunken, and the landscaping, such as the trees and grass, began to die and look abandoned.

Fortunately, the City of Tempe assumed the obligations of operating the cemetery in 1958. After sixty years of private, volunteer organization management, the Tempe Double Butte Cemetery fell under the administration by the City of Tempe. It remains under city ownership to this day.

The Double Butte Cemetery is the final resting place of Charles Trumbull Hayden (the founder of Tempe), Carl T. Hayden (Arizona senator, 1927–69), Dr. Benjamin Baker Moeur (Arizona governor, 1932–36), John Howard Pyle (Arizona governor, 1950–54) and U.S. congressman John Robert Murdock. It is also the final resting place of eleven of Tempe's mayors and many of the town's prominent citizens who played roles in the community's growth over the past century. Many owned homes that are listed in the National Register of Historic Places.

Some of these famous pioneers are known to haunt their former homes or establishments. Could these ghosts haunt the Double Buttes Cemetery as well? Do they use their burial plots as a terminal where they can arrive and go to the places where scores of people have witnessed their presence? In past years, late-night visitors to the cemetery have reported seeing a dark, shadowy figure of a man in a top hat walking through the cemetery parallel with Broadway Road.

Charles Trumbull Hayden's grave lies in the Hayden family plot near the front entrance of Double Butte Cemetery. His son, Senator Carl Hayden, grew up in Hayden's Ferry. He rests in a plot nearby along with Charles Hayden's daughter, Anna.

Farther east, we find the grave of Eliza Teeter. She was widowed at a young age and ran a Phoenix boardinghouse to make ends meet. She died in the back bedroom of the home, which is now called the Teeter House Tea Room. Her ghost has been seen walking through the restaurant. She rests peacefully beside the tomb of her beloved husband.

Grave marker of Charles Trumbull Hayden at Double Butte Cemetery. *Author's collection.*

Recently, the great-granddaughter of Eliza Teeter contacted Debe Branning and told her she had visited Eliza's former home in recent years. "It was wonderful to see the place again," she smiled. "The kitchen still had the same lanolin tiles on the floor. I told them how I use to play jacks on the floor in the kitchen. That same afternoon, I stopped at a Goodwill to do some thrifting. A strange thing happened. Suddenly, I stepped on one jack. I looked around, and there were no other jacks on the floor! It was as though Eliza followed me there and acknowledged our earlier conversation."

Perhaps Eliza Teeter would enjoy a quick game of jacks the next time you visit her grave marker.

Casey Moore's Oyster House has been a trendy bar in Tempe for several years, but it was once the residence of William and Mary Moeur, part of the prominent Moeur family who lived along Ash Street.

Eliza Teeter's grave site at Double Butte Cemetery. *Author's collection.*

The couple both died in the house but passed separately, one in front of the downstairs fireplace and the other in the upstairs bedroom. Reports of dancing ghostly silhouettes, thought to be the spirits of the Moeurs, have been witnessed by neighbors from time to time. The couple lies side by side in the Moeur family plot for an eternal waltz.

As you begin to investigate the ghosts of the Haydens at Monti's La Casa Vieja, Mrs. Teeter at the Teeter House Team Room and the Moeurs at Casey Moore's Oyster House, be sure to include a stop to see their grave sites at the very haunted Double Butte Cemetery and see if they have come home for the night. They just might acknowledge ghost hunters with an "I see you, too."

NIELS PETERSEN HOUSE
1414 WEST SOUTHERN AVENUE
TEMPE, AZ 85282

The Niels Petersen House is a local historic landmark in Tempe and is listed in the National Register of Historic Places. The house is important as the oldest example of Queen Anne–style brick architecture in the Salt River valley. Reverend Edward Decker inherited the house in 1927 and made several modifications to it.

The house is associated with Niels Petersen, a Danish immigrant and prominent local farmer and businessman. It was designed by James Creighton, a well-known Arizona architect. The house was built for Petersen, who came to Tempe in 1871. He developed large landholdings and was the president of the Bank of Tempe, a cofounder of the Tempe Methodist Episcopal Church and representative at the Eighteenth Territorial Legislature (1895–96). Creighton, the architect who designed the home, worked for many years in Arizona and was known for his existing

The Niels Petersen House. *Wikimedia Commons.*

works, such as the Pinal County Courthouse, Old Main (Arizona State University) and the Tempe Hardware building on Mill Avenue in Tempe. The house was added to the National Register of Historic Places in 1977.

Niels Petersen was born on October 21, 1845, to Peder Mikkelsen and Gunder Marie Nisdatter in Vilslev, Denmark, a small farming community. Petersen spent several years in the English merchant marines, which allowed him to travel the world. He immigrated to the United States in 1870.

Petersen arrived in the Salt River valley of central Arizona in 1871; there, he staked a homestead claim and begin farming. The original homestead is currently bordered by Priest Road, Southern Avenue, Alameda Drive and Fifty-Second Street. Construction on a two-room adobe house soon began. Four years later, in 1878, Petersen proudly became a United States citizen and later filed a homestead entry, the next step in permanently establishing himself in the Salt River valley.

In 1884, Petersen married Miss Isabel Dumphy, a teacher at Tempe Grammar School. After they were married, Isabel immediately resigned from her teaching position and moved into the Petersen House. She died during childbirth one year later, in 1885, and their infant son, John Petersen, died within a few months after his birth.

A few years later, Petersen began purchasing the properties that surrounded his homestead claim, expanding his interest in the area. His ranch grew to more than one thousand acres, and soon, Niels Petersen became one of the area's leading producers of cattle and grain.

He was a trustee for the Tempe School District and was a member of the Maricopa County Board of Supervisors, asserting his interest and knowledge in local education.

By the 1890s, Petersen had risen to be one of the Salt River valley's wealthiest and most prominent citizens. In 1892, he made the decision to construct his new Queen Anne–style home. Architect James Creighton was commissioned by Petersen to design the new two-story home that was to be constructed on Petersen's ranch south of the town of Tempe.

While the new home was under construction, Niels Petersen traveled back east to Pennsylvania, where he met his future bride, Susanna Decker. They were married on September 1, 1892. The couple soon returned to the newly completed home in Tempe. The beautiful Petersen House was considered one of the most elegant homes in the valley.

Niels Petersen died at his Tempe home on April 27, 1923, at the age of seventy-eight. As a testament to the respect he commanded in the community, the town's flags were flown at half-mast. All schools and

The Petersens were buried on their property. *Author's collection.*

businesses were closed during his funeral. The funeral was held on the lawn of his country home. Originally buried in Tempe's Double Buttes Cemetery, Petersen's remains were later exhumed and reburied on the grounds of his home, next to the grave of his second wife, Susanna. She, too, died at their home after suffering a long illness on October 13, 1927. You can visit their graves on the grounds of the Petersen House.

Debe Branning and Megan Taylor attended a gardening event held at the Petersen House. A tour of the home was included, so it was a perfect opportunity to explore the home and seek out any possible spirits. Although the docents insisted the house was not haunted, they suggested the pair walk around the second floor. Debe felt a protective energy still watching over the ranch house. It was nothing dark or malevolent, just someone who was still watching over the house.

A blogger wrote,

> *A few years ago, I briefly lived in the house that stands on a small piece of what used to be the Niels Petersen Ranch in Tempe. It has been beautifully renovated as it is in the National Register of Historic Places. It might not be haunted (or it might—who knows), but the house clearly has a very interesting history. Additionally, the former owners are buried on the site, which adds a definite macabre atmosphere. As historic buildings*

The Petersen House serves as a local museum. *Author's collection.*

usually do, the sight of this old mansion put me into a very deep, reflective mood. Though I no longer live there, the house still interests me a great deal, especially as the man who built it helped to form the City of Tempe. Even though I don't live near the house anymore, I am currently writing a paranormal novel that takes place on the former ranch. I have no evidence that the house or the property is haunted in real life, but the history of the locations is incredible to think about either way.

Life, death, history—these people died almost one hundred years ago. The man who helped build Tempe and his second wife are buried there. After all that time, their remains are still there in the middle of a park, which is quite macabre. When I look at their house and graves, I cannot help but try and picture what life was like back then. The Petersens died long before we were born. Things like this old ranch house and these gravestones are the only evidence that they ever existed—and a hundred years from now, those things will be the only proof of our existence as well. The fact that these people are buried in the backyard of their house where they once lived makes it all seem much more macabre to me—and a thousand times more interesting.

Someone else added, "I use to live a street over and encountered many supernatural experiences in the park and in my home on Huntington Drive years ago."

THE FATE OF E.G. FRANKENBURG
TEMOE HARDWARE BUILDING
520 SOUTH MILL AVENUE
TEMPE, AZ 85281

On a warm summer day in June 1899, Mr. E.G. Frankenburg went out to the pasture about a half mile from his house near Tempe, Arizona, for the purpose of catching his buggy horse, a big gray mare he had driven for several years. His ranch was located about two miles south of central Tempe and two miles east, which would put it around Southern Road and Los Feliz Drive. He had a rope coiled around his wrist, and just as he fastened one end of the rope to the animal's head, Frankenburg turned around to talk to an old acquaintance from Globe, Arizona, who was passing by.

While engaged in conversation, several horses and cattle in the pasture crowded up next to the captive horse, biting or in some way frightening her. She turned around, suddenly tightening the rope around Frankenburg's wrist so he could not free himself. He was dragged or pulled along for some distance. He stumbled, and it so happened that the rope was long enough that it landed the unfortunate man behind the mare's hind feet. The frightened horse kicked him several times. Most likely, the first kick was fatal or knocked Frankenburg unconscious.

The horse was not considered a dangerous animal, and as soon as she turned her head and saw her master at her feet, she stopped. Mr. Shields from Globe was finally able to cut the rope and free the horse. But Frankenburg was lying face down, dead.

Frankenburg's body was taken to his house, and an examination showed that his shoulders were broken, his right arm was broken at the elbow, he had several contusions and gashes on his head and a wound on his neck that looked like the horse had stepped on him. He had been dragged about two hundred yards.

Frankenburg had come to Arizona around 1880 to make his home near Tempe. He had at one time or another owned various ranch properties south of town and had been among the foremost citizens of the county. He was one of the directors in the Tempe Canal System.

The old Tempe Hardware building, constructed in 1898. *Author's collection.*

He was a member of the Independent Order of the Odd Fellows and officer in the Grand Lodge. The members of Tempe Lodge no. 8 said, "He was really the leading spirit in the construction of the handsome building owned by the lodge in Tempe."

The Tempe Hardware building is the oldest three-story, brick commercial building that still stands in Maricopa County. Its construction began in April 1898. One of the first businesses to operate out of the first floor of the building was the Abell, Wilbur and Mullen Hardware Company. The International Order of the Odd Fellows commissioned the building and used its second floor for the Odd Fellows Hall.

The building is most recognizable today for its sturdy, red-brick façade and shops and boutiques at the front. It has been home to several clubs, organizations and fraternities.

Frankenburg's leading spirit could possibly be visiting some of his old haunts, such as the location of his ranch southeast of town, the old Tempe Hardware/IOOF building and his family plot at Double Butte Cemetery. A paranormal investigation could be something to ponder in future years.

CAFFE BOA: HAUNTED HALLWAY OF THE HOTEL CASA LOMA
398 SOUTH MILL AVENUE
TEMPE, AZ 85281

Hotel Casa Loma gained a reputation for being the place to stay back in its early days along Mill Avenue, just a few miles south of the Salt River. In 1888, it was known as the two-story Tempe Hotel. But like many of the town's other early wood-framed structures, Hotel Casa Loma was destroyed by a fire in 1894.

Six years later, a new $13,000 "fire-proof" brick hotel was constructed at the same location. The three-story Atwood Hotel, as it was then called, gained popularity until 1902, when a scandal involving its namesake forced another name transformation. Its name was changed to Hotel Casa Loma, the name it carries in records today.

It was advertised in the newspapers as the Sunshine Hotel, however, and its policy was never to charge guests for any days on which there was no sunshine. Knowing the weather in Arizona, I am sure there were not many free days acquired by visitors and early travelers. The hotel had a grand

Vintage Casa Loma Hotel. *Courtesy of Flickr.*

lobby that featured a huge fireplace. Each of its forty-two rooms opened to its own balcony

Hotel Casa Loma became Tempe's premier place of lodging. Famous guests at the hotel included President William McKinley and Buffalo Bill Cody, among scores of others. President McKinley stayed there just months before his assassination in 1901.

The hotel went through successive owners and operators. By 1927, the hotel was in much need of modernization and a facelift. A December 1927 *Arizona Republican* article declared, "[The] Casa Loma Hotel, at one time one of the most popular and fashionable hostelries in the valley, will open shortly after the first of the year as one of the most modern and attractive tourist hotels in the valley."

The popular hotel had been revived once again. The building was converted from its exposed-brick Victorian appearance to the stucco Spanish Revival style that was popular in the late 1920s. The "new" Casa Loma reopened for business on March 17, 1928. It continued to operate as a popular hotel for two more decades.

After World War II, Arizona's population began to boom! Tempe's growth and changing demographics forced the closure of the then nearly half-century-old lodging veteran. It began to function as a residential apartment building.

Mill Avenue was widened as part of the federal highway system in the 1950s, and vacationers in their automobiles began to flock to the desert of Arizona and its majestic saguaro cactuses. The Casa Loma suffered a severe façade cut, and its eastern side was trimmed way back and flanked by large wire mesh screens. In 1984, as part of urban renewal, the venerable National Register of Historic Places–eligible structure was once again restored to its 1928 appearance.

The old Hotel Casa Loma, once a busy hotel on Mill Avenue, has been closed for several years. It now houses Caffe Boa on its ground floor and several modern offices on its second and third floors. Caffe Boa was created in 1994 as part of the fine dining area of the Mill Avenue. Known for its delicious Italian food and fine wine, Caffe Boa is the perfect place to celebrate a special occasion.

Like most hotels, the Casa Loma had its share of accidents and deaths on its premises, the most tragic being the stabbing of a young woman in 1966. The coed had come to the hotel to visit a friend and listen to music in one of the rooms. Sadly, she was murdered outside as she was securing the lock of her bike.

A group of ghost hunters interested in the history and ghosts of the former Hotel Casa Loma gathered in the back room of the Tempe, Arizona restaurant Caffe Boa on Saturday, October 30, 2010. Paranormal investigators Debe Branning and Cindy Lee met the group as they were finishing up their desserts and began telling them the history and mysteries of the Hotel Casa Loma. The historic hotel was built in 1899 to replace the former Tempe Hotel that had succumbed to a fire in 1894. The hotel seemed to have had a checkered history spiced with scandal and glamour.

Some of the employees and diners in the café on the ground floor claim they have heard disembodied footsteps on the levels above them. Another employee saw the apparition of a young girl on many occasions while the building was undergoing renovations.

A former tenant of the building, who lived there when it operated as a hotel in the 1970s, reported,

I lived here in the late 1970s, early 80s. At first, I lived on the second floor in what I believe was the bridal suite. One day, my roommate and I were sitting in the living room in front of the fireplace. Our two cats were sitting on a table in front of us. They both started to growl at the exact same time, focusing on something we could not see. Their eyes became huge, their ears flattened on their heads. It was obvious they had seen something that we did not! After that, I moved upstairs to a studio apartment. I would regularly hear footsteps going down the narrow wood hallway and brushes against my door, but there was no one there.

The small group of twelve walked around outside the building, where they reentered through a separate doorway that led into an office building, the former rooms of the once-grand hotel. They were bedazzled by the

Modern Caffe Boa. *Author's collection.*

beautiful Spanish walnut, wood-carved staircase that formerly graced the old Casa Loma Hotel. The staircase and woodwork in the building are all original and seem to hold a lot of residual energy. Debe and Cindy handed out a variety of EMF meters, thermo scanners and recording devices so that everyone in the group could have a chance to experience the basic tools of a paranormal investigation.

The third floor has been noted as an active spot in the building. In the 1980s, Cindy's former husband was the contractor in charge of the building's reconstruction and restoration. Cindy happened to be in the building when she witnessed the ghost of a young girl. She noted the girl was walking along the edge of the walls inside the doorways of the newly enlarged rooms. Her pathway would have been outside the rooms and in the hallway of the original floorplan. This apparition is a prime example of a residual energy playing out the act of walking the hallways, not knowing the building has undergone renovations. Whether it is the spirit of a hotel guest or of a young girl searching the hotel for her best friend, the spirit upstairs seems to remain on the top floor.

The group sat in the third-floor hallway and conducted a controlled EVP session, which is a somewhat more modern scientific version of the old-fashioned séances from Victorian times. The guests chimed in with some of their own questions and became quite involved in the entire investigation process. After a brief Q and A session, the Caffe Boa ghost hunt and EVP guests ventured out into the streets of Mill Avenue in search of other ghosts that may still roam there.

GHOSTS OF MONTI'S LA CASA VIEJA
100 SOUTH MILL AVENUE
TEMPE, AZ 85281

Monti's La Casa Vieja in Tempe was a dining institution for valley residents for over sixty-five years. The historic adobe hacienda was constructed in 1871 by Charles Trumbull Hayden. Hayden settled in the area to start a flour mill and ferry service for crossing the Salt River, which flowed year round in the early days of the settlement.

It served as the residence of the Hayden family, who nicknamed their home La Casa Vieja. In Spanish, this translates to mean "the old house." It was the birthplace of Carl Hayden, one of the most important people in Arizona history, serving as a soldier and congressman. Early records show there may have been a restaurant in operation at the site as early as the 1890s. It was most likely opened for the comfort of travelers crossing the Salt River on the ferry or those who used the flour mill. The old adobe is one of the city's original pioneer homes and the oldest continuously occupied structure in the Phoenix metropolitan area.

It was located at the north end of Mill Avenue, just a few blocks from Arizona State University, near the banks of the Salt River and now Tempe Towne Lake.

Several proprietors ran the restaurant and bar between the Great Depression era and 1954, when Leonard F. Monti Sr. purchased the property. Realizing the restaurant's historic heritage, he merely added his last name to the establishment, dubbing it Monti's La Casa Vieja. Monti carefully researched the history of La Casa Vieja. He was able to acquire photographs, memorabilia and historic relics to display throughout the restaurant. Senator Carl Hayden (1877–1972) enjoyed making frequent visits to his childhood home and offered several anecdotes and stories about the historic building.

In 1984, the Hayden House was listed in the National Register of Historic Places. Although there have been alterations and additions to the original "casa," a visit to Monti's La Casa Vieja is like stepping into Arizona's pre-statehood days. The old adobe building includes an original latilla mud ceiling in its oldest section.

While noted as a world-famous steakhouse, Monti's La Casa Vieja was also known to be one of Tempe's most haunted locations. It was well known among Tempe-area locals, as well as the other Tri-City visitors.

Monti's La Casa Vieja. *Courtesy of* Ryan's Good Eats.

Many patrons came here not just for steaks and burgers but also to witness one of the ghosts. The restaurant's maze-like structure contributed to its ghostly atmosphere, as diners found it easy to get lost within its halls. Patrons had their cutlery disappear or get thrown off tables, and many guests felt random cold spots or a chill run down the backs of their necks while walking down certain hallways. Considering the building's history and the fact that there were a few deaths there over the years, it is no wonder energies have remained behind—thus leaving a stubborn ghost or two that are reluctant to leave. Some employees felt the ghosts of Charles Trumbull Hayden and his son Senator Carl Hayden were still roaming the rooms of their old casa.

The various rooms in the restaurant had different names, each with their own ghostly ambiance. The Mural Room boasted a giant mural, and patrons have often reported seeing an old cowboy resembling Hayden hanging out there near the room's large painting. The cowboy was said to be friendly, but he was known to disappear in the blink of an eye. The cowboy specter was seen stretched out and relaxing on one of the room's long padded benches. It is said the ghost was decked out in boots and a well-worn cowboy hat. He once slowly faded away as an awestruck busboy

Above: Monti's photographs on historic walls. *Author's collection.*

Left: Monti's well. *Author's collection.*

stood there observing him. Diablo Way was a dark and spooky hallway that seemed to absorb the sound of voices.

The Hayden Room was where Carl Hayden is said to have been born. The sign posted in the Hayden Room was somewhat inaccurate; Carl was born in a smaller, more secluded room beyond the Hayden Room. The room's dimly lit and spooky atmosphere gave many patrons the shivers. Some said they could still feel Hayden's mother struggling to give birth. Others say they simply felt a "weird" feeling upon entering the room, often without knowing about story of Hayden's birth.

The Fountain Room was known to be the most haunted spot in the restaurant. It was also the most popular of all the La Casa Vieja dining rooms. True to its name, the patio-themed room had a large fountain sitting in its middle. On a quiet night, patrons could hear the laughter of children playing near the fountain as they dined. Some say the Arizona chapter of the Illuminati (Free Masons) once conducted their meetings in the Fountain Room.

Staff often refused to do clean-up duty in the Fountain Room. They thought it was a spooky room in any given daylight hour. But after hours, the room became even creepier. Workers claimed they heard laughter and conversations after hours and said the noise came from within the restaurant, as if it was still open for business.

Paranormal activity was noted in the Fountain Room, which was once part of an open courtyard when the Hayden sisters operated their restaurant and tearoom there. It is believed that one of Charles Trumbull Hayden's granddaughters died at a tender age and was buried close to the fountain. Although her remains were moved to Double Butte Cemetery, there have always been reports of children's voices being heard near the fountain. Does the little girl's spirit still come to play at La Casa Vieja? The relaxing courtyard was later enclosed and was one of the larger dining rooms. By day, the large fountain at the end of the room offered the tranquility of the soothing, trickling sounds of moving water. But late at night, the cleaning crews heard laughter and happy children playing near the area of the fountain and refused to enter and clean the room.

Staff members in the spacious restaurant said they heard footsteps and whistling and witnessed flickering lights and cabinets opening and closing. Strange noises were often heard after the patrons left and the employees were preparing the dining rooms for the next day's guests. Some paranormal investigators witnessed the full-body apparition of a woman walking through the rooms of the restaurant. Others heard the tinkling sound of a dinner bell calling the former overnight guests to the dinner table.

Several years ago, members of the MVD Ghostchasers paranormal team decided to go to Monti's for a Valentine's Day celebration. They arrived for a late-evening dinner in the hopes of staying a bit after closing for one of their famous impromptu investigations. It paid off! They spoke to the hostess

The grave site of Senator Carl T. Hayden in Double Butte Cemetery. *Author's collection.*

when they arrived at the restaurant, and she assured them it would be no problem, as the staff was normally there very late.

Just for fun, the group snapped several photographs in the dining room while they enjoyed their romantic dinner and drinks. The atmosphere in the building began to change, and they were certain they had gained the energies' curiosity. While waiting for dessert, Shiela and Debe left the table under the pretense of using the restroom. Out in the hallway, they chatted with several waitresses who showed them where they had previously seen unexplained shadows or felt the presence of someone stepping closely behind them as they worked.

The restaurant was nearly empty. The ghost hunters asked if they could step into the notorious Fountain Room, then vacant and quiet, to see if they could record some EVPs on the recorder they were carrying in a bag. The hostess escorted the six ghost hunters into the room. They each took a seat at a table near the fountain, which was decorated with a delightful little cherub, and conducted a brief EVP session.

Eventually, the patient hostess, anxious to go home, escorted the group to the front door. The staff was ready to lock up and finish up the evening's work. The team of ghost hunters walked out to the parking lot and played back the old-fashioned tape recording they had just made inside of Monti's Fountain Room. They listened closely to the grind of the tape recorder. Suddenly, they looked at one another at the same time. On the recording device, they could hear a faint giggle, as if it was coming from a child. They were almost positive there were no small children in the area that evening, but one can never be sure. Did the MVD Ghostchasers have an encounter with the spirit of Sally Hayden?

Jamie Veik of PAPS (Phoenix, Arizona Paranormal Society) added,

> *Before this historic steakhouse gave way to the high-rises in downtown Tempe and shut down, we were given the opportunity to investigate this location a few times, and we were not disappointed. The building still stands, as it houses the original home that Arizona Pioneer Carl Hayden was born in, so it shall remain there until the city figures out what to do with this historic gem. Every room in the building gave us so much evidence of ghosts roaming this location. We had examples from the kitchen, different rooms within the restaurant, conference rooms and the fountain that stands inside: tons of EVPs, EMF fluctuations and Spirit Box responses, as well as visible shadows reported by multiple team members. The darkest thing captured was an EVP that said, "Tonight, I'm gonna sleep with your soul." And the coolest EVP was, as I was panning a night vision camera on some pictures on the wall, a male voice says, "It's too loud," followed by another man that said, "It's not loud, only in the beginning." That was a very cool class A EVP. We think that was a residual response, but there are intelligent spirits there as well. It is an incredible place.*

Sadly, Monti's La Casa Vieja officially closed on November 17, 2014. The group of paranormal friends decided to visit the spirits one last time to celebrate investigator Colleen Sulzer's birthday. It was bittersweet but very special at the same time. You could almost smell the aroma of the restaurant's famous rosemary-scented Roman bread. Monti's La Casa Vieja building remains vacant until the spirits are revived.

Even after the closure of the building in 2014, La Casa Vieja remained haunted. Urban explorers and ghost hunters have often wandered into the building or kept a vigil on the grounds. The cowboy ghost still hangs out, and the fountain in the Fountain Room still echoes with the eerie sounds of disembodied children. Most who have explored the abandoned La Casa Vieja say the same thing: though it is empty, it still sounds like a restaurant. They heard cutlery scraping against the dishes, laughter and conversations, almost as if the restaurant never closed. Listen for the dinner bell.

THE ANDRE BUILDING: UPROAR AND COMMOTION
401 SOUTH MILL AVENUE
TEMPE, AZ 85281

The Andre building once housed the popular Irish pub known as Rula Bula. The two-story Andre building is located on the north end of Mill Avenue in Tempe. It is significant for both its design, which combines Victorian and Neoclassical elements, and history. It was originally built in 1888 to house the saddle business owned by Robert G. Andre. Unfortunately, the structure was destroyed by a fire in 1899. Andre rebuilt the two-story building on the same site and was back in business in 1900 with Mr. C.G. Jones. The Jones family owned the property from 1912 to 1977. This historic structure housed the Price Wickliffe's Furniture and Undertaker business from 1912 to 1929. It was also home to a newspaper, the AZ Cotton Growers Association and a U.S. post office. The Andre building was a Masonic lodge for the local Free and Accepted Masons, as well as other fraternal organizations. Its second floor was used as a boardinghouse and apartment complex. It was entered in the National Register of Historic Places in 1979.

Robert G. Andre was born in France in 1847 and raised and educated in Germany. He came to the United States in the early 1870s and made harnesses and saddles for the troops stationed at Fort Grant. He later moved to Phoenix and then to Tempe, where he opened his business on Mill Avenue. Andre then left for a trip to the eastern part of Arizona and was expected to be gone for several weeks. He caught a ride on the local stagecoach and

The Andre building once served as a lively Irish pub. *Author's collection.*

was then involved in an accident near the Highland Canal, just east of Mesa. He had been lying on top of the load when the stage struck a small chuck hole in the road. He fell, and one wheel passed over his body, severely crushing his right shoulder. His injuries were not considered severe at first, but several hours later, on July 2, 1904, he died from his wounds at his Tempe home. Andre was buried in the AOUW section of the Pioneer and Military Memorial Park Cemetery in Phoenix. Could Andre be the ghost that haunts the building bearing his name and the old Rula Bula Pub?

Rula Bula was taken from the Irish Gaelic saying "*ri ra agus ruaille buaille*," which translates to "uproar and commotion." That certainly described the celebration and good fortune experienced each time

View of the Andre building. *Author's collection.*

guests frequented the pub! Uproar and commotion also clearly describe the poltergeist activity in the pub.

The décor of Rula Bula paid tribute to Mr. Andre, creating a saddle style saloon. In Ireland, a merchant's shop would often double as a neighborhood pub. The staff at Rula Bula often said they felt watched by unseen eyes as they worked. The waitstaff said they occasionally felt as though someone was standing behind them, but when they turned around, nobody was there.

One of the bartenders had experiences with the mysterious strangers on more than one occasion. It usually occurred in one area at the corner of the bar. One evening, at about 11:00 p.m., the bartender and an older-looking guest were the only people sitting at the bar. The patron ordered a drink, and they struck up a conversation. The bartender turned his back for just a moment to put away some glasses, and when he spun back around, the mysterious customer had vanished, leaving his full drink behind.

Late one night, the same bartender started a discussion with another odd sort of customer who asked about the fires that had taken place in the Andre building. Besides the fire of 1899, a second fire that occurred one hundred years after the first, in 1999, almost destroyed the building as renovations of the former pub began. Just as the customer stated that he believed nobody was injured in the fires, a glass popped up two feet into the air and dropped to the floor, shattering into several pieces. Is the ghost of the Andre building someone who died in the earlier fires?

Whether the spirit is the ghost of R.G. Andre, a fire victim, a residual guest left behind from the building's undertaking business or an energy from the many antiques that once decorated the pub, you will experience Arizona's old Wild West within the walls of the notable building. A new business will soon grace the historic Andre building. They say a true Irish pub is distinguished by its *craic*, an Irish term referring to positive interactions among people through conversation, stories and music. You will find this and more amid the uproar and commotion of the Andre building.

CASEY MOORE'S OYSTER HOUSE
850 SOUTH ASH AVENUE
TEMPE, AZ 85281

This popular eating and drinking establishment sits within a Colonial Revival home with Victorian details. The home was constructed in 1910 by William and Mary Moeur on the northwest corner of Ninth Street and

The historic Moeur family home. *Courtesy of the Tempe History Museum.*

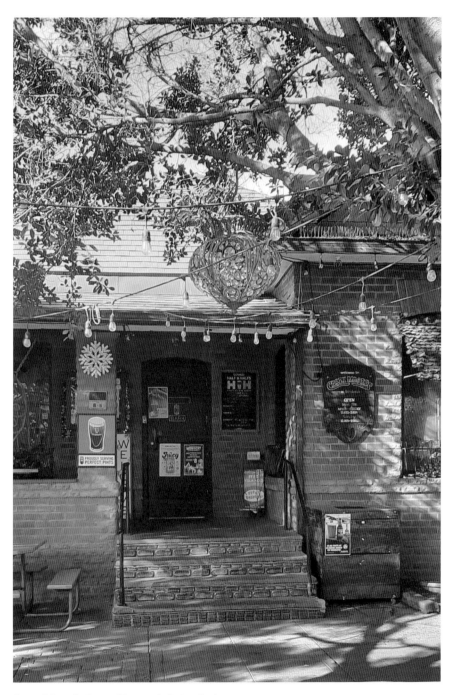

Casey Moore's Oyster House. *Author's collection.*

Ash Avenue, near downtown Tempe. It was made of brick, and its owners have tried to keep the décor in line with the home's original stylish features. The two-story house is a perfect example of a Victorian home that was transformed to a classic box-style home. It is very comfortable yet small inside. It boasts a sturdy copper bell-cast roof that could trigger some of the unexplained paranormal that occurs there. This quiet Tempe neighborhood housed several members of the Moeur family, and many of the relatives lived within blocks of each other. Aunts, uncles and cousins literally lived down the street or just around the corner from each other. The children played in one another's backyards and visited each other's homes regularly.

William Moeur was a well-respected businessman in Tempe. His brother Dr. Benjamin Moeur served two terms as the governor of Arizona (January 2, 1933–January 4, 1937). Eventually, both William and Mary Moeur died in their home. William died of a brain hemorrhage on Christmas Day 1929, near the fireplace in the living room area downstairs. Mary died two decades later, on July 10, 1948, in the upstairs bedroom (the Blue Room).

In the years that followed, it was rumored that the historic home became a brothel for a short period. It did function as a boardinghouse for ASU college students and perhaps became a popular spot for friends to come by, entertain themselves and possibly end up spending the night. It is suspected that around 1966, a young girl who was staying at the house was brutally murdered. It's suggested there was a quarrel in the upstairs bedroom. Many say the girl was strangled or killed with a knife. Although this urban legend has never been proven true, could it have been kept a secret among friends? In 1973, the Ninth and Ash bar and restaurant opened, later to be converted into an Irish pub called Casey Moore's Oyster House in 1986. Casey Moore's Oyster House has gained a reputation for being a pearl in this historic Tempe neighborhood on Ash Avenue.

Debe Branning and the MVD Ghostchaser team were asked to do a series of investigations with the news reporting team at Arizona Central. Their first official scheduled investigation was at Casey Moore's Oyster House. They met with the news team after dining hours in the upstairs area of the restaurant, the notorious Blue Room. Eight members of the investigating crew were on hand to set up cameras and recording devices and monitor and record any data or findings. The Arizona Central crew brought their reporters, camera crew and a psychic named Gertie to round out the paranormal investigative merger.

The MVD Ghostchaser crew were asked to enter the small, private dining areas above the bar first. Immediately, the group felt as if someone unseen was anticipating their arrival. The air in the room seemed to grow thicker, almost like a slowly swirling energy. The hair on Mark Christoph's arms stood up on end.

Psychic medium Gertie came into the house next, not knowing the stories of its ghosts and hauntings. As she walked up the stairs to the upper dining rooms, she felt the strong presence of someone hiding from them. Later, when the paranormal team played back their digital recording devices, they heard an EVP recording that said, "Hi!" It was imprinted as Gertie approached the upstairs rooms. One of the camera crew members heard laughter in her ear, and another felt her head being stroked in the upstairs hallway. The group was ready for a busy evening!

As visitors can imagine, many ghost stories about Casey Moore's have circulated throughout the years. One of the most common tales is that neighbors have seen a woman dancing or a loving couple performing a series of ballroom dances in front of the upstairs window. Other observers have seen lights turn on and off upstairs all on their own. Motion detectors go off on their own accord. Neighbors have called the police, and when officers searched the building, they found no intruder.

One of the MVD Ghostchasers, Gary Tone, was a former Tempe police officer in the 1980s. He remembered responding to a possible intruder call at Casey Moore's. The officers started their search on the ground floor and made their way slowly to the upstairs rooms. There are several small attic-hiding closets and doors in these rooms. Gary, being the smallest officer, was elected to climb into the tiny crawl spaces, flashlight in hand, in pursuit of the phantom burglar. Again, Tempe's finest came up empty handed!

Employees of Casey Moore's have reported encountering a mischievous spirit that rearranges and tips over the furniture in the upstairs dining room. They have also heard ghostly laughter filtering through the building. When going upstairs to prepare for diners, they find table settings rearranged or food or utensils thrown onto the floor. Some evenings, this is accompanied by the sounds of laughter or giggling as the playful spirit creates a ruckus. No matter how orderly the staff arranges the dishes and tables at closing time each evening, they will find them in disarray the next morning. The bartenders have reported liquor bottles disappearing, being tapped roughly on the shoulder or seeing rows of glasses falling at the same time off a rack. They have heard their names being called out by an unseen voice and have had their neckties yanked by unseen hands.

The owners have also heard their names being called out. One of the owners keeps a collection of spirit photographs that have been taken by

Casey Moore's haunted bedroom window. *Author's collection.*

patrons and other ghost hunters, and they will proudly display them if asked. They have seen and heard children playing upstairs when there are no children there. It's said you can see them faintly, but when you look again, they are gone.

Former roomers from the building's boardinghouse days have returned to the restaurant and talked about seeing the face of a stern-looking girl standing behind them in the mirror as they shaved. Many describe her as having fair skin and long, dark hair. They refer to her as "Sarah, the ghost." Many have seen the spirit of a woman floating in a hall doorway upstairs. The specter has a blank stare on her face and suddenly fades away into the darkness. Visitors report having an uneasy feeling that they are not alone, which is accompanied by a slow-moving, cold breeze.

On the night of a news channel investigation, the MVD Ghostchasers waited patiently until the bar closed and the smoke from the cigarettes finally dissipated. The film crew had left a few hours prior, and now, there were just three of the investigating crew taking some last photographs using night vision video cameras and digital cameras. Suddenly, a lamp on a nearby table shut off on its own. Although they discovered it was set on a timer, the lamp was not set for the correct day or time when it went dark. The team felt they could not claim this as real paranormal data and immediately debunked the event.

Around 1:45 a.m., Debe and Liz Brown felt like they were walking out of balance in the upstairs dining room. They felt they were being pulled, as if magnetized, to the east end of the room. Mark stepped inside and immediately felt nauseated. There was a definite change of atmosphere from earlier in the evening. At 2:15 a.m., they set the cameras back up in that room. Liz noticed the overhanging edge of the tablecloth swishing as if someone had walked by and brushed against it. Later, they packed up their cameras and equipment and all smelled a faint lilac perfume.

Debe likes to recall when she and the MVD Ghostchasers came close to becoming ghosts themselves while on a second investigation at Casey Moore's.

We were filming a paranormal segment with a crew from Telemundo. They asked us to drive our hearse around the block and slowly pull in front of the restaurant. We hopped in the hearse and began our trip around the block. Suddenly, as we began to cross the railroad tracks on Ninth Street, the train signal began to ring and the train whistle was blowing. I know our hearts skipped a beat! We survived the railroad crossing, but as we pulled in front of Casey Moore's, the hearse began to overheat, and a cloud of smoke began to billow from under the hood! The camera crew and awaiting patrons thought it was merely a special effect and cheered us on! It's a wrap!

If you are craving oysters and seafood, Casey Moore's is the place to go! Be sure to request the Blue Room upstairs. Hang on to your forks and knives and don't let the spirits tip over your chairs!

EISENDRATH HOUSE
1400 NORTH COLLEGE AVENUE
TEMPE, AZ 85281

During the Roaring '20s and 1930s, traveling to Arizona was still considered traveling out to the Wild West. Folks expected to see cowboys and Indians dressed in clothing they saw their favorite western stars don in the Saturday matinées. Well-to-do easterners and mid-westerners were looking for new winter vacation destinations where they could travel and experience the untamed Southwest and learn the culture of the Native Americans.

Rose Eisendrath was the widow of a Chicago glove manufacturer. She was one of the many affluent Chicago residents who spent their winters vacationing in the Southwest. Eisendrath came, as many others did, to discover the culture and history of the Southwest, making Arizona the place to get away during the cold winter months.

After being turned away and refused accommodations at a valley resort due to her Jewish heritage, Rose Eisendrath acquired forty acres of land

Eisendrath House is nicknamed Lomaki, which means "pretty home." *Author's collection.*

in the hills above the Salt River in North Tempe on April 23, 1930, and commissioned a home to be built by architect Robert T. Evens, the son of a Chicago friend.

The house was nicknamed Lomaki, which translates, in Hopi, to "pretty home"—and indeed it is! Rose hosted vacationing guests at Lomaki every winter for six years until her death on Christmas Eve 1936.

The Eisendrath House pool. *Author's collection.*

The house boasted 5,500 square feet of living space, a dumbwaiter, a citrus grove and a swimming pool. The house was designed to entertain. All were welcome at Lomaki, including the hotel manager who had turned Rose away. The house was passed along from owner to owner for several years until "the pink house on the hill" eventually became neglected and abandoned.

Fortunately, the City of Tempe purchased the land and began the task of restoring the grand home. It was turned into the Eisendrath Center for Water Conservation, and it offered free water conservation classes for nearby residents. The Tempe History Museum currently manages the Eisendrath House. It serves as a museum and location for meetings and receptions. The Eisendrath House was listed in the National Register of Historic Places in 2016.

Occasionally, Eisendrath House hosts open houses and historic tours, where the public is invited to step back in time and experience what it was like when the home was a showcase for visitors to Arizona. Debe Branning and Megan Taylor took a tour of the grounds in early 2019 and could feel the presence of a welcoming spirit watching over the visitors from a window. Does Rose still send out a welcoming invite for those who wish to stop and visit?

Debe returned to Eisendrath House for another tour in 2023. She asked one of the docents if anything paranormal or out of the ordinary ever happened in the home. As Debe rode the elevator with them to the second floor, the young docent recalled the day when she opened the door to the lift, only to find a rattlesnake awaiting her. That could be very scary, but it's not a ghost tale.

Another docent, however, believed the ghost of the Eisendrath House was connected to the drowning of a more recent owner in the home's pool. Gloria Gould Barker, age thirty-seven, died tragically on August 15, 1943, when she slipped on a wet tile at the swimming pool, hit her head and drowned. Some suggested foul play. The swimming pool was drained, bricked and cemented over.

Eisendrath relatives have described visiting the house in their youth and experiencing glasses falling out of cupboards, listening to phantom cocktail parties and seeing the Christmas tree and garland strewn about the floor on Christmas morning. Keep in mind, Rose Eisendrath passed away in the home during the Christmas holidays.

Although the ghosts and hauntings have not been confirmed by the staff, the home's views of the Superstition Mountains to the east are absolutely spooktacular!

THE ARIZONA HERITAGE CENTER AT PAPAGO PARK
1300 NORTH COLLEGE AVENUE
TEMPE, AZ 85281

The Arizona Heritage Center opened in 1992 and is located at Papago Park. It is one of the state's leading historical museums. Visitors can stroll among historic artifacts from Arizona's past, present and future to explore the rise of the Tri-Cities and more. Discover World War II through the eyes of Arizona residents and prisoners of war. Explore the culture and diversity of the Southwest.

The center's exhibits focus on the history of central Arizona from its territorial days through World Wars I and II; it also explores the state's encounters with UFOs and the modern growth of the valley. There is an excellent archive library in which guests can research historical events and early Arizona pioneers.

Docents and archivists of the museum have experienced hearing the footsteps of unseen guests walking down the hallways or up and down the stairways. They have heard the chatter of men, women and children in various areas of the building.

"We have heard a woman greet us as we enter the building with a cheery 'Hello!' when nobody else is in the museum," historian/archivist Jenn Merry recalled. "It startled us at first, but now we are used to it."

Another employee, Dennis, is one of those fortunate people who can see and hear spirits. He has had encounters with the ghosts at the museum quite often. "I have seen the children—the little boy and girl—and they enjoy the area where some of the pioneer toys are displayed. They are very mischievous and like to move things around or hide items from us."

Dennis has seen the center's ghostly architect, as well as some of phantom soldiers. He believes that sometimes, the center gets busy with spirit activity, and he tries to appease some of these lively spirits when he can. He believes one soldier longs for a cigarette from the pack of Lucky Strikes on display in the military section. "I leave him a cigarette near the display once in a while to calm his energy down."

Dennis continued, "I have seen the woman who wanders about the building as well. We believe she could be the spirit of Hattie Mosher, a larger-than-life local character who spoke her mind and fought often with old city hall over issues she was strongly for or against! Eventually, she became a 'riches-to-rags' story and wandered the streets of Phoenix. Her

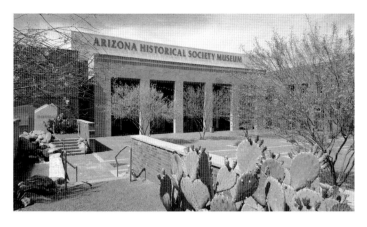

The Tempe Heritage Center's courtyard. *Courtesy of the Tempe Historical Society.*

family donated several items to the museum, and she could be keeping a watchful eye over them!"

Hattie's presence is usually detectable by the fragrance of freshly cut roses.

Debe Branning visited the museum one afternoon in February 2024. It had been a while since her last visit, so everything was refreshing and new. She slowly walked to each display on the second floor, taking in all the history to see if she felt anything unusual or paranormal. Jenn Merry escorted her down to the archives storage area and showed her Hattie Mosher's daughter's diary and other historic items.

She approached the display, which was set up to resemble architect Louis C. Hill's 1912 office. He was a key engineer in the development of Arizona's Roosevelt Dam. Debe noticed the display featured a set of his tools enclosed under glass on a wooden desk. Hill's spirit made it known that he did not like his tools being touched by anyone. Debe backed away.

Debe then headed over to the military section and began reading the information about a display of German army helmets. One helmet especially caught her eye, and she stared at it for several minutes. The message she kept getting was that the spirit of a German soldier was in the room, and he felt the display was very disrespectful.

"Strange you should mention that," K.D. Forgia, the center's activity director said.

Just last night, we had a group of navy officers meeting up here for a private gathering. About an hour before their arrival, I came upstairs to turn on the lighting. The lights began to flicker, and the entire lighting system went out for about thirty minutes. Perhaps the ghostly soldiers were not excited about the reveling of the evening's naval guests. After all, there was a German

POW camp just down the road, located near the intersection of Curry Road and College Avenue from 1942 to 1944.

Debe suggested that perhaps the museum's grounds are active due to its proximity to Papago Park and the site of early Hohokam villages. There is some evidence that the Hohokam used and recorded the position of sunlight shining through the openings in the red rock formations to mark the seasons, notably the equinoxes and the solstices, making these sacred grounds and very powerful sites. "After all, your 'next-door neighbors' at the Eisendrath House have spirits, too! They have the spirit of Gloria Gould Barker who accidently slipped on the tiles at the pool, hit her head and drowned."

"Oh, really?" K.D. Forgia was wide-eyed. "I have seen a spirit of a woman walking in the building drenched from head to toe. Now it all makes sense."

Sometimes spirits attach themselves to favorite items. No harm is intended, but they do create an uneasy feeling just the same. Perhaps an overnight investigation, or a "night at the museum," is in order.

TEMPE O'ODHAM RUINS

In the fall of 2023, the Tempe city planner and archeologists concluded the makeover of East Eighth Street after the street project had to be put on hold in 2019, when it discovered that important ancient artifacts in a roughly 1,300-year-old Native village were found buried beneath a portion of the project's construction site.

The city project was meant to spruce up the roadway between South Rural Road and South McClintock Drive with pedestrian-friendly walking pathways. Tempe had to check for historic artifacts on the site before it could start construction. This is something required by local, state and federal law whenever a project of this magnitude is started. This led to an amazing prehistoric discovery.

The village dated to at least 850 CE, according to the Tempe archeological report. The researchers believe it was once the home to members of the ancestral O'Odham tribe until about 1450, or about two hundred years before the founding of New York City.

Its inhabitants lived in comfortable homes with plaster floors. They had constructed a nearly four-mile-long canal system to transport water from the Salt River to a field just north of the main settlement. The O'Odham farmed maize, cotton and squash. They were avid traders who acquired pottery from as far away as Black Mesa, a site nearly two hundred miles northeast of Tempe.

The most remarkable find of the excavation was an exceptionally rare adobe multistory building that dated to the 1300s. Only six such structures have ever been found in the Phoenix Basin. It was the most significant building found, as it was the center of community life in the past. This discovery was thought to be a once-in-a-career opportunity. In most cases, these structures had already been destroyed by the progress of time and weather.

The building had at least seven interior living spaces on its ground floor and may have had at least two additional floors above that. Descendants of the village's original habitants believe it was a ceremonial house called a va'aki. It was a residence for important extended family members in the village, a gathering place for community leaders and perhaps a location for community religious ceremonies.

Debe Branning was not surprised when she heard about the ancient settlement.

I lived less than a half mile away, just east of McClintock Drive, for ten years in a small tri-plex apartment. Strangely, I never felt alone. I often saw a tall, dark Native man standing in my closet or in various rooms of the apartment. Clothes hangers would rattle in the closet, cupboards would bang as I sat at the kitchen table paying the bills and lights would flicker on and off. One evening, I invited a date over for dinner. Suddenly, a mirror that was hanging in the living room fell off the wall and shattered! It had been hanging in the exact same spot for six or seven years! As you can imagine, the potential suitor never returned! I never felt any negativity but more as though he was there to protect me.

Branning later learned about some artifacts that were found a few miles east of the apartment when the 202 Freeway was under construction at University and Price Roads. Things were beginning to make sense! "A few years later, I was invited back to a gathering at a different complex in my old neighborhood," she noted. "I just had to ask the resident, 'Have you ever had any unexplained things happen in your apartment?' They looked at me and asked, 'You mean the tall Native American man?' I smiled and nodded, 'Yes!' I wonder if he is still there."

A HAUNTING AT FOUR PEAKS BREWERY
1340 EAST EIGHTH STREET SUITE 104
TEMPE, AZ 85281

The Pacific Creamery Company was owned and operated in the building on Eighth Street between 1907 and 1924. It made a brand of evaporated milk called Lily Milk. The manufacturers would remove about 60 percent of the milk's water content and then heat and sterilize it while it was canned. This process led the cream to have a slight caramel color. Lily Milk was advertised and famous for being white, just like regular milk.

This popular product was essential to early Arizona pioneers. In 1915, the creamery produced 60 percent of all the milk consumed in the state. It is impossible to say how much of that was Lily Milk, but since residential refrigerators were not in full service yet, it is guessed it was a large amount. The sale of Lily Milk wasn't limited to Arizona. The Pacific Creamery Company shipped the milk to nearby states and south of the border to Mexico. By 1917, it was also being shipped to war-torn Europe. Lily Milk,

The Borden Creamery building. *Wikimedia Commons.*

produced by local Arizona cows was sent to American troops fighting in World War I.

Around this same time, Tempe residents voted in favor of banning alcohol. The first vote occurred in 1908, and by 1911, the sale of hard alcohol in the city was banned for good. Ironically, the voting took place inside the Tempe Creamery Building, the same spot where alcohol is brewed today.

The building is one of Tempe's most historic landmarks and has a long history of housing essential businesses for the area. It is the fourth-oldest commercial building in Arizona. In 1892, it was home to the Tempe Creamery and an ice plant, and later, it housed F.A. Hough's Ice Factory. Next, in 1907, it became Pacific Creamery, the largest Arizona plant with over sixty employees. It became Borden Creamery in 1927 and had a Spanish revision to its building design. It is noted that in 1953, the plant was shut down and abandoned. Four Peaks Brewery and Restaurant has occupied the space in 1993.

The owners of the one-hundred-year-old brick building that houses the original Four Peaks Brewery found the building had paranormal activity right from the start. They heard weird noises from up in the rafters. Tools they left in one section of the brewery at the end of a shift would move and end up in an entirely different spot overnight. Some of the employes interreacted with the spirits. One worker noted he had conversed with a ghostly apparition during his work hours.

After doing some background research on the history of Eighth Street and the Four Peaks Brewery building, it was easy to see that area has seen its share of tragedy. There were accidents on the nearby roadway to the south of the building as well as on the train tracks to the north.

There were also several accidents that occurred inside and outside of the creamery. The *Arizona Republic* noted that on June 26, 1907, an accident near the creamery resulted in a serious incident. Shortly before noon, a man who was driving a team of mules hitched to a top buggy met with an accident at the Pacific Creamery Company plant that soon became serious for him. As he passed the plant, the noise of the machinery frightened the mules, and they started to run. He was able to hold them at first. But soon, the pole of the buggy's rig dropped from the neck, and a moment later, it struck a high place on the ground. The rig was overturned in an almost summersault. The driver was hurled to the ground and hit the back of his head. He suffered a deep gash in his scalp, and his back was badly hurt. A doctor took a serious view of the accident and considered the injured man to be in very bad shape. He was then brought to town and placed under good care at the Olive Hotel.

Little could be learned about the victim of the accident aside from the fact that he had been working for some time with Waterhouse and Casner on that company's thresher. His name was thought to be Lane Donnelly, and it was understood that he had cattle up in the mountains. Before coming to Tempe, he had made Glendale his headquarters.

The night fireman at the Pacific Creamery Plant was burned in an explosion on July 10, 1908. He was standing in front of the fire box door when he added more oil and the gas ignited. The man's shirt caught on fire. His hair and eyebrows were burned off, and his face was blistered. He suffered painful but not serious injuries.

Sadly, another victim of an accident near the plant was a dog. On October 1, 1904, the dog was rambling through the Tempe Creamery and condensed milk plant when, while passing the fly wheel of the engine, it thought it could save time by going through it instead of around it. The wheel was in rapid motion at the time. The dog went through the wheel alright but made several revolutions before reaching the other side. When it at last made a connection with the wheel and landed some twenty feet away, the poor dog (bless its soul) did not survive.

Another accident occurred at creamery while an engineer was fixing a light beam. It fell and killed a cat. Today, workers and guests often see a ghostly black cat.

Paranormal teams such as CLS Paranormal, AZPIRS (AZ Paranormal Investigation and Research Society), MVD Ghostchasers and several others have done investigations of Four Peaks Brewery. Debe Branning and Megan Taylor stopped in at Four Peaks Brewery to take a mini tour of the site one weekday afternoon. The manager was happy to escort them through the building and related several of its more interesting stories while he escorted the ladies on a ghost walk of the historic building.

"What do you think of this room?" He asked as they entered one of the largest brewing rooms." A lot of people will not even enter this room. They feel it to be very dark and say it has a heavy presence of a former employee. It has been seen in this room."

The women walked into the room and looked round. The room has a very weird affect, they noted, almost like walking in a room that has that carnival fun house feeling. There was nothing dark or evil, but the room definitely feels a little off, which makes it hard for folks to concentrate while they are inside. The room seemed quite busy with spirit energy. The manager walked the women to several rooms, and it was amazing to them what a large operation the brewery had become!

Four Peaks Brewery barrels. *Courtesy of Megan Taylor.*

"There was a paranormal show here filming a month ago," the manager said. "They filmed in several areas of the building." It was later revealed that the show was *Ghost Adventures*, featured on the Discovery Channel.

One of the main ghosts seen or heard at the brewery is the spirit of Victor Vogel, who was a former superintendent (or general manager) of the Borden Creamery. Vogel worked in the building for nearly twenty years, starting in 1927. Although Victor eventually left the creamery business and passed away in 1972, it seems his spirit has returned to one of his favorite places of business.

Four Peaks' head brewer, Andy, met with the spirit of Victor Vogel face to face just a few months before the brewery officially opened. Not only did he see the apparition, but Andy also spoke with Victor! The spirit told Andy how he nearly died in an accident many years ago in the spot where the new owners had built a cooler. Victor's family confirmed the story was true. This interested the founders so much that they decided to hold a séance to find out more!

Vogel started to communicate with Andy and told him, "I almost died over there [pointing to the spot where the blade mixer stood]." Andy turned around, and the man had disappeared. Another employee brought in a newspaper article about a gentleman who almost died there in the 1930s. Vogel crouched down to the base of the machine to avoid the dangerous blades. He yelled for help until someone came to rescued him. Victor Vogel died in 1995.

Other ghosts that have seen in the building include a tall, gray man and the spirit of a little girl. A spirit called Anthony has also been seen, but he is not fond of visitors and generally hides out in one of the closet areas. His spirit does not like people in his workspace. He is always watching the workers and visitors. The little girl is usually seen in the barrel room, standing back in one of the corners.

The employees hear strange voices and echoes, and some have heard their names called out. Some have been pushed or touched, while others

The Four Peaks
Brewery building.
*Courtesy of Megan
Taylor.*

have witnessed shadowy figures moving along the walls. They have heard
banging coming from the fertigation room and tanks. They have checked
these rooms, only to find nobody in sight.

Where do all these spirits come from? No one knows. But Eighth Street
runs through an area that has been inhabited for the last 1,200 years. The
Native Akimel O'odham people lived in this area, and two Indigenous
cemeteries were discovered just down the road from the brewery. This is
also the site where the first white and Mexican settlers lived in Tempe.

Stop in for dinner, have a drink or take a tour of the brewery. I think you
will find the facility is "lager" than life!

Debe's 1972 Cadillac hearse. *Courtesy of Cindy Lee.*

Paranormal Resources: Teams and Tours

Arizona Desert Ghost Hunters: www.adghosthunters.com

AZ Ghost Adventures: www.azghostadventures.com

AZ Paranormal: info@AZParanormal.com

AZ Paranormal Investigations and Research Society: www.azpirs.com

Crossing Over Paranormal: www.thecopscrew.com

East Valley Paranormal: www.evpinvestigates.com

Friends of the Other Side: www.friendsoftheotherside.org

Ghost Hunters of Southern Tucson: www.facebook.com/groups/2468619340062334/?ref=share

Ghost to Ghost Arizona: www.ghosttoghostaz.org

MVD Ghostchasers: www.mvdghostchasers.com

Phoenix Arizona Paranormal Society: www.phoenix-arizona-paranormal-society.com

Phoenix Ghost Tours: https://phxtours.com/ghost-tour

Phoenix Haunted History Tours: marshallshore@gmail.com

Rydables: www.rydables.com

Southern Arizona Scientific Paranormal Investigators: www.SASPI.org

BIBLIOGRAPHY

Anderson, Lisa A., Alice C. Jung, Jared A. Smith and Thomas H. Wilson. *Mesa*. Images of America. Charleston, SC: Arcadia Publishing, 2008.

Arizona New Times. "Sales from the Darkside: Chandler's Terror Trader's Is a Little Shop of Horrors." August 11, 2022.

Arizona Republic. "Explosion of Gas Man Badly Hurt." July 10, 1908.

———. "Rode the Fly Wheel." October 1, 1904.

———. "Tempe Hurt in a Runaway." June 26, 1907.

AZ Central. "Who's Buried in Mesa Cemetery?" August 29, 1922.

Blanton, Shirley R. *Tempe*. Images of America. Charleston, SC: Arcadia Publishing, 2007.

Branning, Debe. *Arizona's Haunted Route 66*. Charleston, SC: Arcadia Publishing, 2021.

———. *Dining with the Dead*. Phoenix, AZ: American Traveler Press, 2017.

———. *Grand Canyon Ghost Stories*. Malvern, PA: Riverbend Publishing, 2012.

———. *The Graveyard Shift*. Phoenix, AZ: American Traveler Press, 2012.

———. *Haunted Globe*. Charleston, SC: Arcadia Publishing, 2022.

———. *Haunted Phoenix*. Charleston, SC: Arcadia Publishing, 2019.

———. *Sleeping with Ghosts*. San Marino, CA: Golden West Publishers, 2004.

City of Mesa. "Mesa Public Schools." Mesa, AZ. 1978.

Clark, Victoria. *How Arizona Sold Its Sunshine*. Sedona, AZ: Blue Gourd Publishing, 2004.

Crago, Jody A., Mari Dresner and Nate Meyers. *Chandler*. Images of America. Charleston, SC: Arcadia Publishing, 2012.

Mark, Jay, and Ronald L. Peters. *Buckhorn Baths and Wildlife Museum.* Charleston, SC: Arcadia Publishing, 2017.

Mesa Tribune. "Santa Claus Coming in Airplane." December 9, 1932.

Mullaly, Katie, and Patrick J. Ohlde. *Finding Ghosts in Phoenix.* Atglen, PA: Schiffer Publishing, 2010.

Pascoe, Jill. *Arizona's Haunted History.* Niwot, CO: Irongate Press, 2008.

Robson, Ellen. *Ghosts of the Grand Canyon State.* San Marino, CA: Golden West Publishers, 2002.

Spears, Linda, Frederic B. Wildfang and the Tempe History Museum. *Tempe. Then & Now.* Charleston, SC: Arcadia Publishing, 2010.

ABOUT THE AUTHOR

Debe Branning has been the director of the MVD Ghostchasers, a Mesa/Bisbee, Arizona–based paranormal team, since 1994. The team conducts investigations of haunted historical locations throughout Arizona and has offered paranormal workshops/investigations since 2002. Debe has been a guest lecturer and speaker at several Arizona universities and community colleges, science fiction and paranormal conferences, historical societies and libraries.

Her television appearances include an episode of *Streets of Fear* for FearNet.com (2009); an episode of Travel Channel's *Ghost Stories* about haunted Jerome, Arizona (2010); and an episode of *Ghost Adventures*, "Old Gila County Jail and Courthouse" (2018). As a paranormal journalist, she has investigated haunted locations—including castles, jails, ships, inns and cemeteries—and has taken walking ghost tours in the United States, England, Scotland, Ireland and Mexico. She has been the guest of the Historic Hotels of the Rockies and U.S. tourism departments in Carlsbad, Salem and Biloxi.

Debe is the author of *Sleeping with Ghosts: A Ghost Hunter's Guide to AZ's Haunted Hotels and Inns* (2004), *Grand Canyon Ghost Stories* (2012), *The Graveyard Shift: Arizona's Historic and Haunted Cemeteries* (2012), *Dining with the Dead: Arizona's Historic and Haunted Restaurants and Cafés* (2017), *Haunted Phoenix* (2019), *Ghosts of Houston's Market Square Park* (2020), *Arizona's Haunted Route 66* (2021), *Haunted Globe* (2022), *Haunted Schools of Arizona* (2024) and a series of three children's books in The Adventures of Chickolet Pigolet series: *1. The Bribe of Frankenbeans*; *2. Murmur on the Oink Express*; and *3. You Ought to Be in Pig-tures* .

FREE eBOOK OFFER

Scan the QR code below, enter your e-mail address and get our original Haunted America compilation eBook delivered straight to your inbox for free.

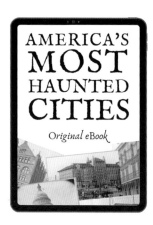

ABOUT THE BOOK

Every city, town, parish, community and school has their own paranormal history. Whether they are spirits caught in the Bardo, ancestors checking on their descendants, restless souls sending a message or simply spectral troublemakers, ghosts have been part of the human tradition from the beginning of time.

In this book, we feature a collection of stories from five of America's most haunted cities: Baltimore, Chicago, Galveston, New Orleans and Washington, D.C.

SCAN TO GET
AMERICA'S MOST HAUNTED CITIES

Having trouble scanning? Go to:
biz.arcadiapublishing.com/americas-most-haunted-cities